IMAGES
of America

EISENHOWER'S
GETTYSBURG FARM

This August 9, 1967, photograph documents the Eisenhower farm just months before it was donated to the National Park Service. The allée of trees leads to the circular drive in front of the home. Behind the house, the putting green with sand trap, flagpole, and privet hedge surrounding the clothes dryer are evident. In the foreground are a martin birdhouse, floribunda rose bed, incinerator, vegetable garden, playhouse, greenhouses, and teahouse. The US Secret Service found the battlefield observation tower in the upper right a safety concern, closing it whenever Eisenhower was here as president. (EL68-361-4, US Marine Corps, A.J. Parsonese.)

ON THE COVER: Dwight and Mamie Eisenhower pose for photographers in the circular flower bed behind their home on September 16, 1956. (EL72-1868-35, NPS.)

IMAGES
of America

EISENHOWER'S GETTYSBURG FARM

Michael J. Birkner and Carol A. Hegeman
with Kevin Lavery
Foreword by Susan Eisenhower

ARCADIA
PUBLISHING

Published by Arcadia Publishing
Charleston, South Carolina

Library of Congress Control Number: 2016954001

For all general information, please contact Arcadia Publishing:
Telephone 843-853-2070
Fax 843-853-0044
E-mail sales@arcadiapublishing.com
For customer service and orders:
Toll-Free 1-888-313-2665

Visit us on the Internet at www.arcadiapublishing.com

For the Eisenhowers

CONTENTS

FOREWORD

Adjacent to some of our nation's most hallowed ground, the Eisenhower farm is a historic site of another century. Its modesty and setting betrays the historical importance of what happened at the farm nearly a century after the Battle of Gettysburg. During Dwight D. Eisenhower's presidency, the Gettysburg, Pennsylvania, farm served as a place of refuge and regeneration for the former general and sitting president, especially during the tense and difficult days of the Cold War. Less than 100 miles from Washington, DC, Eisenhower's farm allowed him to unwind or to use this bucolic setting as a place to entertain World War II comrades and postwar world leaders, such as Prime Minister Winston Churchill, Soviet premier Nikita Khrushchev, and French president Charles de Gaulle.

The white brick house is the first one Ike and Mamie ever owned. It was also their first true home. They had spent countless years of their married life abroad, apart, or on the move. As our authors note, Eisenhower also relished the idea of running a farming operation that would leave "a piece of ground better than he found it."

The farm not only became a focal point for family gatherings, it also served as the White House during the president's recovery from a heart attack in late 1955.

For students of history, clues to Ike and Mamie's lives are everywhere. Visitors can easily get a sense of the personalities of the president and first lady—from the most formal rooms to the most casual of them and from the official gifts to the keepsakes exchanged among family members. The house today is a veritable time capsule of life from the 1950s to the 1960s.

There are no two authors better suited to introduce you to the Eisenhower farm than Dr. Michael Birkner and Carol Hegeman. Dr. Birkner is a preeminent Eisenhower scholar who has written numerous works on the president and, as a professor at Gettysburg College, has always had a close relationship with the Eisenhower farm site. Carol Hegeman spent 34 of her 42 years of federal service working at the Eisenhower National Historic Site, receiving a superior service award from the Department of the Interior for her dedication to preservation of the site and extensive work on collecting oral histories from those connected to the farm. In the pages that follow, Birkner and Hegeman give you a glimpse at this unassuming, yet historic presidential home, which I hope will compel you to come to the farm and see it for yourself.

—Susan Eisenhower

ACKNOWLEDGMENTS

This book would not have been possible without the help of the staff at Eisenhower National Historic Site, who allowed us access to the photograph files and archive materials. Kathy Struss, the audiovisual archivist of the Eisenhower Presidential Library, was also essential in providing and identifying photographs. The Gettysburg College Library Special Collections staff assisted with photographs. Brian Kennell, Will Lane, and Lauren Roedner came through for us in a pinch. The Dwight D. Eisenhower Society provided essential funding to cover photograph duplication, license costs, and other needs. Paul Shevchuk and Daun Van Ee offered expert comments on an early draft of our text.

Photograph Credit Abbreviation Key

ENHS	Eisenhower National Historic Site Photograph Collection
EISE	Eisenhower National Historic Site Archival Collection
NPS	National Park Service
HFC	Harper's Ferry Center
EL	Eisenhower Presidential Library
NARA	National Archives and Records Administration
HSTL	Harry S. Truman Presidential Library
USDI	US Department of Interior
USA	US Army
USN	US Navy
SC	Signal Corps
AP	Associated Press
GT	Gettysburg Times, Gettysburg, Pennsylvania
LS	Lane Studio
ZS	Ziegler Studio
EC	Eisenhower Collection, Eisenhower Presidential Library
GCSC	Special Collections/Musselman Library, Gettysburg College
ACHS	Adams County Historical Society, Gettysburg, Pennsylvania
PRC	Paul Roy Collection
BEC	Barbara Eisenhower Family Photograph Collection
ANC	Ann Nevins Collection
MJMC	Mary Jane McCaffrey Collection

INTRODUCTION

In the course of his storied life, Dwight D. Eisenhower hung his hat in many different communities, but he called only two of them "home"—Abilene, Kansas, where he grew up, and Gettysburg, Pennsylvania, where he retired. Eisenhower's Gettysburg address was a farm fronting on Millerstown Road three miles south of the town center—an easy jaunt to the Peach Orchard, Little Round Top, and to the ground Gen. James Longstreet's corps trod on the fateful afternoon of July 3, 1863.

Eisenhower and his wife, Mamie, did not purchase their Gettysburg home until relatively late in life. After a weekend house-hunting excursion in the fall of 1950, the Eisenhowers bid on the 189-acre Allen Redding farm. They knew the Gettysburg community well from previous experience. As a West Point cadet, "Ike" Eisenhower had joined his compeers on a staff ride to Gettysburg in 1915 and posed for a photograph in front of Christ Lutheran Church on Chambersburg Street. Three years later, now married to the former Mamie Doud and father to their little boy "Icky," Eisenhower returned to Gettysburg to command Camp Colt, which was located on the battlefield south of town. There, he would help train thousands of recruits in tank tactics and deal with a major crisis in the form of a flu pandemic that beset his charges.

It was in Gettysburg that Mamie Eisenhower, as one biographer has put it, first "shared her husband's problems and successes." Mamie created a comfortable home life for her husband despite the need to move on two occasions during their eight months in Gettysburg. She was absorbed in her parenting duties for Icky while her husband was at the camp but found time occasionally to tour the battlefield with Ike as he pointed out the places where Lee had miscalculated and Union forces had taken advantage of these errors. This happy early experience together later encouraged the Eisenhowers to choose Gettysburg as their retirement home.

As it turned out, the Eisenhowers' Gettysburg address proved something more than a retirement aerie. Even before serious renovations began on the old farmhouse surrounded by land Eisenhower intended to leave better than he found it, he launched a successful campaign for the presidency. And only months after the property was fully habitable as a vacation residence during Eisenhower's tenure in the nation's highest office, the Gettysburg farm took on special import as the place where the president recuperated from a serious heart attack in 1955 and conducted the nation's business.

For the next five years, the Gettysburg farm proved itself a welcome retreat from the White House fishbowl and, in Ike's case, a heavy daily schedule of meetings and all-too-frequent crisis management. Ike took a special interest in his small Angus cattle herd, which grew to national prominence on the show cattle circuit. Golf, skeet shooting, bridge games, and oil painting all added to his enjoyment. The Eisenhowers' greatest pleasure lay in hosting son John, John's wife, Barbara, and their four children on occasional weekends and holidays. That connection would grow during the later presidential and retirement years, as John assisted his father on the White House staff and with his memoirs. John and Barbara purchased a house practically a stone's throw from Ike and Mamie's home and moved the family to Gettysburg in 1959, providing ample opportunities for David, Anne, Susan, and Mary Jean Eisenhower to get to know their grandparents.

The Eisenhower farm as a historical site, made possible by the Eisenhowers' deed of gift to the American public in 1967, lacks the grandeur of George Washington's Mount Vernon or the exquisite appurtenances evidenced at Thomas Jefferson's Monticello. The Eisenhower home offers a window for visitors into comfortable middle-class living. Visitors of a certain age will notice material culture and decorative elements common to that era, right down to the pink-tiled bathrooms that Mamie helped popularize.

One

From Abilene to Gettysburg

Growing up on the wrong side of the tracks in Abilene, Kansas, did not hamper young Dwight David Eisenhower's zest for life, nor did it limit his dreams. His parents, David and Ida, raised their six sons to embrace hard work and aspire to lead meaningful lives. All did so, not least Dwight, whose rough-and-tumble boyhood reads like something out of a popular novel.

A bright and vivacious youth, Ike Eisenhower participated in the whole run of recreational opportunities available in Dickinson County in the early 20th century, not least of them playing baseball and football. He was smart enough at school to be encouraged by one teacher to work out Euclid's theorems on his own, and Eisenhower's high school yearbook predicts he will become a history professor at Yale.

Eisenhower loved reading and discussing history, to be sure, but he took a different path that would lead him to make significant history. An appointment to West Point in 1911 broadened his horizons and opened new opportunities to see America and the wider world. Though he chafed at what he considered silly rules and never hit the books as seriously as he should have, Ike loved his life at West Point and took much from his experience there. The Army life that followed took him to several dozen geographically dispersed postings and increased responsibilities that ultimately transformed him into an American icon. Among the most meaningful early postings were San Antonio in 1915, where Eisenhower met the pert 18-year-old Mamie Doud, and Gettysburg in 1918, where he commanded a tank training camp. In Gettysburg, Eisenhower showed his mettle dealing with the flu pandemic that touched down there.

Eisenhower was a natural leader. At Gettysburg, he devised new means of teaching his charges the latest military technology and tactics, entertained visiting military brass, and forged healthy relations with local elites in Gettysburg. Above all, the young officer took pleasure in his domestic life with Mamie and their son Icky, who was the light of the Eisenhowers' lives.

Dwight David Eisenhower grew up in the well-known crossroads community of Abilene, Kansas, the third of seven sons born to David and Ida Eisenhower. Ida made sure that her boys learned to garden and do all the household chores, rotating duties each week. Pictured are, from left to right, Dwight, father David, Arthur, Earl, Milton, Edgar, mother Ida, and Roy. Paul, not pictured, died as an infant. (EL62-319.)

The Eisenhower family moved into this home in 1898. With just three upstairs bedrooms, the home was cramped, but in 1900, when grandfather Jacob moved in, two first-floor bedrooms were built. Jacob died in 1906, and two years later his bedroom was converted to a bathroom. After Ike left home, a new kitchen, pantry, and enclosed back porch were added. (EL73-451-7.)

If ever there was a boy who enjoyed the outdoors it was Ike Eisenhower, as depicted in his informal memoir *At Ease: Stories I Tell to Friends*. When not in school or doing chores at home, fishing, hunting, and pickup football were among Ike's favorite recreations. This photograph shows him camping out with Abilene friends around 1904. (EL64-165.)

As a high school student, Eisenhower excelled in competitive athletics, most notably football and baseball. His passion for baseball ran deep enough that, if his grandson David is to be credited, he even played semipro baseball under an assumed name before matriculating at West Point. Here, Ike is pictured, third row, second from right, with the Abilene High School baseball squad around 1908. (EL66-483.)

Growing up in a household with limited financial resources, Ike and his brothers came up with various strategies for securing college educations. In Ike's case, after working full-time to help pay his brother Edgar's tuition at the University of Michigan, he pursued a free education courtesy of Uncle Sam. Rejected for being overage at the Naval Academy, he secured an appointment to West Point. Here, Eisenhower is in Chicago, en route to the academy in June 1911. (EL64-388.)

Eisenhower's West Point experience helped shape the man he became. He was, as he readily admitted, not the most dedicated student, but he loved West Point culture and accepted the rituals and chores of the academy without complaint, including stints on guard duty, as pictured here with two unidentified fellow cadets. (EL63-514-64.)

Taken on the steps of Christ Lutheran Church as part of his staff ride to Gettysburg with his fellow cadets in May 1915, this photograph is the first document connecting Eisenhower to the community that 35 years later would become his adopted hometown. One can only speculate what the experience of traversing the great battlefield meant to Eisenhower. Clearly, according to his memoirs, it was inspiring. He is pictured in the third row, immediately on the left of the right handrail. (EL63-365, Tipton.)

"He was the handsomest man I ever saw," Mamie once observed about the West Point graduate she first encountered in Texas in 1915, when she was 18 years of age and Eisenhower was 25. Ike was equally smitten with Mamie's sparkly blue eyes and saucy personality. After an eight-month courtship, they were married in her home in Denver, Colorado. This wedding portrait, dated July 1, 1916, captures the appeal of the young couple. (ENHS2101, PRC.)

Captain Eisenhower's first independent command was at Camp Colt, the Army tank training camp located on the Gettysburg battlefield in 1918. British officers came to advise him on tank training techniques, and Eisenhower later wrote, "Thus began my connection with allies." Eisenhower is seated with US Army colonel William H. Clopton and two British officers, Lt. Col. F. Summers and Maj. Philip Hamond, at Camp Colt headquarters. (EL63-584-1.)

Eisenhower found housing in Gettysburg so Mamie and son Doud Dwight, nicknamed "Icky," could join him. This photograph, taken in the back yard of the Alpha Tau Omega fraternity house, shows their second of three homes during Ike's eight-month posting in Gettysburg. As Ike later wrote, "It was fun to have the chance to see my son growing up and spend the evenings with my wife." (EL62-340-2.)

The view in these rare photographs of Camp Colt, which trained almost 10,000 soldiers, is looking south from the west side of Emmitsburg Road. The camp was located on the fields of Pickett's Charge on the battlefield. Note in the upper left background the Pennsylvania Monument, which had been completed and dedicated only five years earlier. Farther in the distance, the Round Tops are visible. The camp was located one mile south of Gettysburg's town center. This was a totally

mechanized camp with vehicles, including trucks, cars, and motorcycles; barracks buildings; latrines; mess halls; tents; and even an inground swimming pool, located below the famous Copse of Trees. These photographs were combined into one by the National Park Service staff at the Harpers Ferry Interpretive Design Center for use on a wayside exhibit. (NARA, USA111-SC-15526 and 111-SC-15527, NPS, HFC.)

At Camp Colt, Eisenhower was assigned to train soldiers in using a new weapon, the tank. But the camp had no tanks. Improvising, Eisenhower set up motor and telegraphy schools and mounted machine guns on flatbed trucks to practice firing from a moving vehicle. Finally, one French Renault tank arrived. Here, infantry practice advancing behind the cover of the tank as it maneuvers at the site of the Bliss farm barn, which burned during the Battle of Gettysburg. (NARA, USA111-SC-15531.)

Eisenhower poses in 1919 at Camp Meade, Maryland. After the war, the Tank Corps was assigned to Camp Meade. There, Eisenhower met George Patton Jr. They had similar views on tank tactics and became good friends. In 1920, after a 15-month separation, housing was finally available and Mamie and Icky rejoined Ike. But shortly into the new year, Icky died of scarlet fever. As Eisenhower wrote, "This was the greatest disappointment and disaster in my life." (EL62-286-3.)

Two

WHERE GLORY WAITS

Late in the 1930s, Eisenhower and his younger brother Milton, then serving the Roosevelt administration, attended a Washington cocktail party at which Milton told guests that his brother was "going places" in the military. "Well," one listener responded, pointing to Eisenhower's status as a major, "if he plans on going places, he had better get going soon." There were, in fact, relatively few opportunities to excel and advance in the small peacetime Army between 1919 and 1940. Americans were focused on internal affairs and hoped the two oceans could serve as a buffer from international upheavals and war.

All the same, Dwight Eisenhower's career between World War I and World War II was eventful and, from the standpoint of personal growth, meaningful. In 1922, he was fortunate to be posted to Panama, where he came under the tutelage of Gen. Fox Conner, who put him through a personal graduate education in history, philosophy, and military strategy. It was Conner who recommended Eisenhower for the Fort Leavenworth Command and General Staff School, a rigorous program where his protégé flourished and graduated first in his class.

Among Ike's further postings, duty in Europe with the Battlefield Monuments Commission and two tours with Gen. Douglas MacArthur (one in Washington and one in the Philippines) were among the most important. Eisenhower excelled in everything he did. By 1940, he was in the sights of Army chief of staff George C. Marshall, who tested Ike in various ways—most notably with command responsibilities in the 1941 Louisiana Maneuvers—and watched Eisenhower consistently rise to the challenge.

Advanced by Marshall past more senior officers, Eisenhower earned his first general's star in 1941. By 1944, he had four and was chosen by Pres. Franklin D. Roosevelt for the job of supreme commander of Allied forces in Europe. A master of human relations, Eisenhower managed a talented but squirrelly group of Allied military commanders with consummate skill. He also forged strong working relationships with President Roosevelt and British prime minister Winston Churchill. The latter was sometimes a trial but backed Eisenhower when the hard decisions had to be made.

By 1945, Eisenhower was the best-known and most popular American military figure, identified as the "people's general" and the man who crushed the Nazis. Feted with enthusiasm across America, he had, indeed, gone places.

"B" – Off the road

Less than a year after the end of World War I and his reassignment to Camp Meade, Maryland, Eisenhower found himself, briefly, stopping in Gettysburg again—having volunteered as an observer to join the first US Army Transcontinental Motor Truck Convoy in 1919. The 81-vehicle convoy left from the Ellipse just south of the White House, traveled north to Gettysburg, and then headed west on the new Lincoln Highway. The trip lasted from July 7 to September 6, a total of 62 days before the convoy arrived in San Francisco, California. Much of the road was unpaved. Bridges broke and had to be rebuilt, vehicles got stuck in mud or ran off the road, and equipment broke down. Eisenhower documented his trip in a series of photographs with his handwritten notes, two of which are shown here. (Above, EL81-17-16, EC; below, EL81-17-41, EC.)

East Wyoming.

Eisenhower's years in Panama were both trying and valuable. With the death of their son Icky of scarlet fever in 1921, Dwight and Mamie's marriage was tested as never before. The birth of John Sheldon Doud Eisenhower in 1922 proved a balm to the Eisenhowers. This photograph captures them at the baby's christening at the Doud family home in Denver in September 1922. (EL81-17-43.)

Gen. Fox Conner, Eisenhower's superior during his Panama years, was a powerfully influential mentor, offering Eisenhower the equivalent of a graduate education in philosophy, history, and military strategy. In 1922, it was Conner's privilege to confer on Eisenhower the Distinguished Service Medal for the younger man's service at Camp Colt. (EL62-332.)

THE GENERAL SERVICE SCHOOLS
Fort Leavenworth, Kansas

18 June, 1926.

SUBJECT: Class Standing.

To: Major Dwight D. Eisenhower, Inf.,

The Commandant directs that you be informed that your final standing in the Command and General Staff Class, 1925-1926, of ....245 members, is number ....1....; the percentage attained by you is 93.079 per cent.

For your information, your standing by months is given below:

October ....14......
November ....9.......
December ....4.......
January ....4.......
February ....3.......
March ....4.......
April ....3.......
May ....3.......

J. G. PILLOW,
Lieutenant Colonel, Cavalry (D.O.L.),
Secretary.

1025—G. S. Schs., Fort Leavenworth—4-30-26—556

General Conner recommended Eisenhower for the Fort Leavenworth Command and General Staff School—a key training ground for future Army leaders. Eisenhower had not distinguished himself academically at West Point, but at Fort Leavenworth his marks were strong and kept improving, and as this document indicates, when final class standing was calculated, he finished first in a class of 245 officers. (ENHS2643, LS27755-1.)

Abilene remained the emotional magnet for the Eisenhower brothers well into the 1940s. In this 1926 photograph, taken on the porch of the family homestead, Eisenhower, then a major in the Army, reunited with his parents and siblings. From left to right are Roy (pharmacist), Arthur (banker), Earl (electrical engineer and media executive), Edgar (attorney), David (father), Milton (then in the consular service), and Ida (mother). (EL67-631.)

From 1927 to 1934, the Eisenhowers spent most of their time in Washington, DC. Ike served on General Pershing's Battle Monuments Commission staff writing a guidebook on the World War I battlefields. He attended the Army War College and then spent a year in France with Mamie and John touring battlefields to revise his guidebook. Returning to Washington, he went to work for Army chief of staff Gen. Douglas MacArthur. (EL63-340-2.)

Eisenhower was posted to the Philippines from 1935 to 1939 as Gen. Douglas MacArthur's right-hand man. The experience provided an acute awareness of Japanese ambitions in the Pacific. Working for MacArthur was at times vexing but also valuable as Eisenhower weighed leadership models. Attending a formal dinner in 1938, Eisenhower, left, talks with Jean MacArthur, while Mamie is seated between MacArthur, right, and US high commissioner to the Philippines Paul McNutt. (EL62-312.)

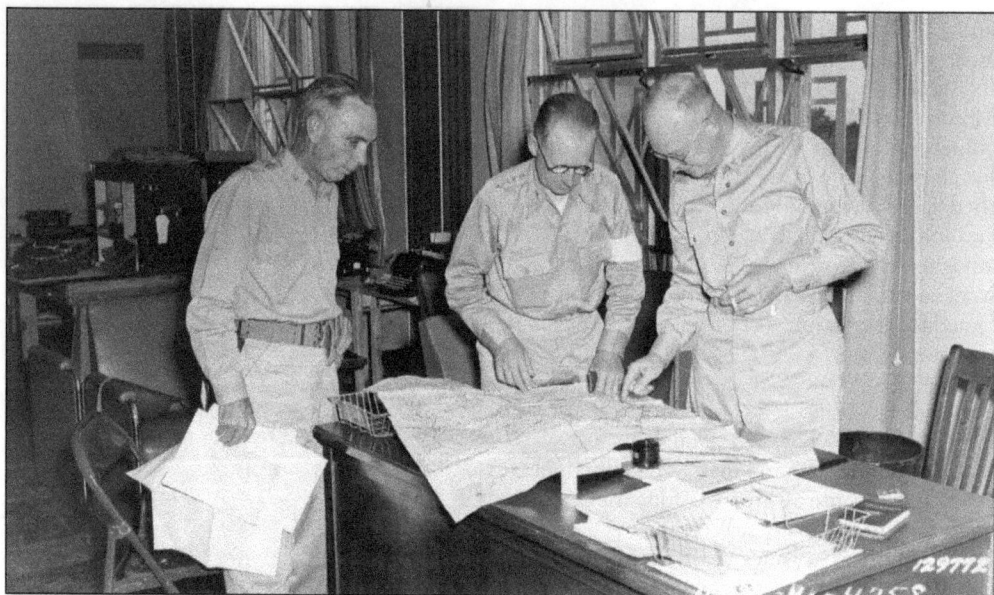

In August 1941, Colonel Eisenhower, now chief of staff to Gen. Walter Krueger, participated in the Louisiana Maneuvers. His leadership of the 240,000-man Third Army "invasion" of Louisiana was immensely successful. *New York Times* military correspondent Hanson Baldwin wrote that if the exercise had been a "real war," the Second Army "would have been annihilated." Army chief of staff George C. Marshall took note. Here, Col. George Barker, Lt. Gen. Lesley McNair, and Eisenhower study a map for the maneuvers. (EL64-57-6, USA.)

In wake of the Japanese assault on Pearl Harbor in December 1941, General Marshall advanced Eisenhower through the ranks past dozens of more senior officers. By June 1943, when this photograph was taken at Allied headquarters in Algeria, Eisenhower held the temporary rank of full general and would soon direct the invasion of Sicily in July and Italy in September. In December 1943, Eisenhower was named supreme commander, Allied Expeditionary Forces in Europe. (EL63-542, USA.)

By January 1944, Eisenhower was in Great Britain to assume command of the planned invasion of France. He increased the size of the invasion force, supported deception plans for the Allied landing site, and ensured that all units were as prepared as possible. Here, Eisenhower observes armored maneuvers with Air Chief Marshal Sir Arthur Tedder and Gen. Sir Bernard L. Montgomery on March 1, 1944. (EL65-314-1, USA.)

This iconic photograph of Eisenhower speaking with paratroopers (Company E, 502nd Parachute Infantry Regiment) was taken on June 5, 1944, just prior to the D-day assault on German positions in Normandy—known as Operation Overlord. The soldier immediately facing him is 1st Lt. Wallace C. Strobel of Michigan. Later, Strobel recalled that Ike was talking about fly-fishing. Airborne casualties were expected to be as high as 75 percent. In reality, they were much lower. (EL65-325, USA SC194399.)

US troops debark from their landing craft for the beaches at Normandy, France. The D-day landings were the largest amphibious invasion ever, with about 170,000 soldiers, sailors, and airmen involved in the initial attack. The invasion was daunting and costly but successful. (EL71-247, US Coast Guard.)

By 1944, Ike was the face of the American army in Europe and possibly the most recognizable public persona in America aside from Pres. Franklin D. Roosevelt. Ike's image was used to encourage participation in war bond drives, as exemplified by this poster. Note the four stars. Ike was promoted to general of the Army and received his fifth star on December 20, 1944. (EL89-14-149.)

Eisenhower pioneered a new style with his tight-waisted "Eisenhower jacket," as shown in this photograph taken in Normandy in the summer of 1944. It was patterned on the British battle jacket and meant to be smart-looking, functional, and comfortable. Ike urged adoption of the shorter jacket in a May 5, 1943, letter to Gen. George C. Marshall. Issuing of the "Wool Field Jacket, M-1944" in the European theater began in November 1944. (EL63-92, USA.)

One of the most challenging of Eisenhower's tasks as supreme allied commander lay in coordinating with British and French military leaders and dealing with prima donnas—notably George S. Patton—in his own ranks. Of all the individuals with whom he worked, Bernard Montgomery ("Montgomery of Alamein"), pictured to Ike's left in France in the autumn of 1944, caused Eisenhower the most heartburn. For his part, Gen. Omar Bradley, on the right, was a valuable if occasionally unreliable associate. (EL66-699-290, USA.)

Eisenhower knew how to manage up, as well as down. One of his most taxing but fruitful relationships was forged with British prime minister Winston Churchill, who sometimes second-guessed Eisenhower but in the crunch stood by him. Here, the two men confer at Supreme Headquarters, Allied Expeditionary Forces in England in 1944. (EL68-640, USA SC.)

Victory was sweet. Ike celebrates with his staff, holding the surrender signing pens in a "V" shape on May 7, 1945, in Reims, France. From left to right are Soviet major general Ivan Susloparov; British lieutenant general Sir Frederick E. Morgan, chief of staff to the supreme commander of the Allied Expeditionary Forces; Lt. Gen. Walter Bedell "Beetle" Smith, General Eisenhower's chief of staff; Capt. Harry Butcher; General Eisenhower, supreme Allied commander; and Air Chief Marshal Arthur Tedder, Royal Air Force. (EL71-316-4, USA, Moore.)

Few successful generals have received the kind of heartfelt and tumultuous greetings on arrival home that Eisenhower enjoyed. This photograph captures Ike hailing an adoring crowd in New York City as part of a ticker-tape parade in June 1945. (EL77-18-416, USA.)

Three

ROAD TO THE
WHITE HOUSE

What does a man who has reached the mountaintop by age 55 do for an encore? That was the question facing Dwight Eisenhower at the close of the Second World War, but it does not seem to have disturbed his sleep or equanimity. He had jobs to do, first as chief of staff overseeing demobilization of millions of American GIs, then preparing the American military for its Cold War responsibilities. In 1947, he took time off to write his war memoir *Crusade in Europe*, which became a national best seller and for the first time put the Eisenhowers in a financial comfort zone.

At several junctures, Eisenhower suggested that he would be pleased to close his post-military career with a small college presidency. None called him, but Columbia University did. From 1948 to 1951, Ike served Columbia as its president, reorganizing its administration, raising substantial sums, and creating the American Assembly, bringing experts together across a wide spectrum of vocations to discuss the most pressing issues of the day.

During his years at Columbia, Eisenhower devoted roughly a day a week to high-level national security meetings in Washington, where he contributed to the shaping of Harry S. Truman's signature "containment" policies. In 1950, with the North Atlantic Treaty Organization (NATO) stumbling and the communist threat growing, Truman called on Eisenhower to return to active service as commander of SHAPE (Supreme Headquarters, Allied Powers, Europe) to create an effective allied military force.

From his base in Paris in 1951 and early 1952, Eisenhower worked with the leaders of the 12 NATO nations to organize their military forces. At the same time, he hosted a steady stream of Republican leaders and party activists who urged him to stand for the presidency. Scholars debate how much Eisenhower orchestrated his advent as a politician, but there is no doubt he was enormously popular. That popularity fueled the Eisenhower nomination struggle against "Mr. Republican," Sen. Robert A. Taft of Ohio, the Republican frontrunner in 1952. But Eisenhower surpassed Taft at the convention, and after running a vigorous whistle-stop campaign in the fall, decisively defeated Democrat Adlai Stevenson of Illinois for the presidency.

During this period, the Eisenhowers began thinking about putting down roots. By 1950, they were persuaded that Gettysburg was the place for them. In the fall of 1950, the Eisenhowers paid $40,000 for the Redding house and farm—the first and only residence that would be truly their own.

On May 27, 1946, Eisenhower returned to Gettysburg for the first time in nearly three decades, to accept an honorary degree from Gettysburg College. Here, the general stands at attention as college president Henry W.A. Hanson extols his virtues. Ike then addressed 90 graduates in the Majestic Theater, highlighting challenges facing the rising generation and his confidence in America's youth. (GCSC, GEI_0777.)

In 1946, Eisenhower succeeded his mentor, George C. Marshall, as Army chief of staff. His main charge was to oversee the demobilization of a great military machine. By 1947, however, relations with the Soviet Union were growing increasingly tense, and Eisenhower was one of the fathers of a policy of "containment." Here, he is caught by a photographer in Nome, Alaska, in 1947 on an inspection tour. (ENHS3954, Miles A. Caughey.)

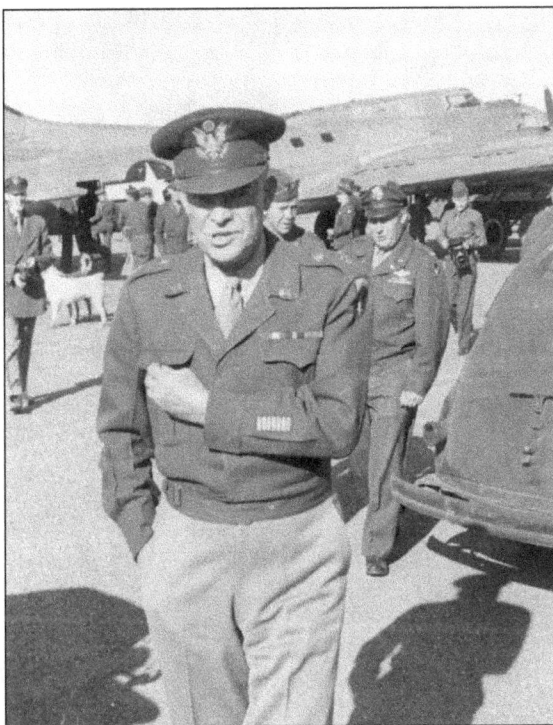

With the war's end, Ike finally had opportunities to relax and unwind, including a chance to reunite with his brothers on a fishing trip in 1946. This photograph captures a light moment with his brothers, from left to right, Arthur, Milton, Earl, and Edgar. The basis for their hilarity pictured here? Earl had just sat on a fishhook. (EL65-65.)

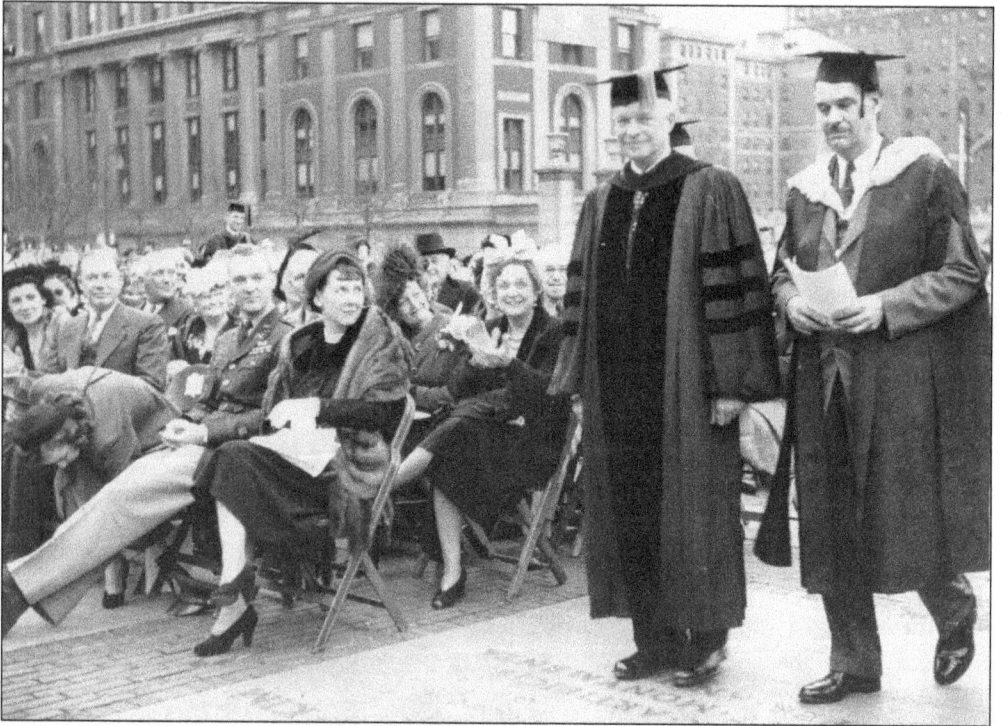

Asked about his plans after the military, Eisenhower said he would like to serve as president of a liberal arts college. None called him, but in 1948, he was offered—and quickly accepted—the presidency of Columbia University in New York City. Before taking up his duties, Ike completed his memoir *Crusade in Europe*, which became a national best seller. He received a lump-sum payment for *Crusade in Europe* that gave the Eisenhowers a nest egg for the first time. On October 12, 1948, Ike is shown at his inauguration as Columbia's president, escorted by Albert Jacobs, while Mamie and John watch the procession. (EL63-185-11.)

It is no surprise to learn that during his presidency of Columbia University Eisenhower, a lifelong football fan, periodically visited his squad's practice fields and attended Ivy League football contests. Here, he observes a practice along with Columbia's coach and football legend Lou Little. (EL66-827-2, Columbia University, Manny Warman.)

PRESIDENT EISENHOWER'S FARM

Looking ahead to life beyond Columbia University, the Eisenhowers began house hunting by 1949. Their happy experience in Gettysburg during World War I and Ike and Mamie's friendship with George and Mary Allen, who owned a farm just south of town, led them to purchase, for $40,000, a seven-room brick farmhouse on 189 acres adjoining the Gettysburg battlefield—the Redding farmstead. This postcard depicts the site around 1952 before major renovations commenced. (ENHS1587B, Mike Roberts, L.E. Smith.)

One of the appealing features of the Redding property was its brick bake oven, located in the summer kitchen visible to the right of the brick house around 1953. Another was the mature trees immediately surrounding the farmhouse. The Eisenhowers planned to fix up the house and move right in. However, an engineering study told a different story. Logs under the brick facing were rotten, necessitating a major renovation. (ENHS2905, LS.)

These photographs, both taken in 1952, show the Eisenhower farm in different seasons of the year. The large Pennsylvania bank barn built in 1887 housed 25 dairy cows. Anywhere from 500 to 600 chickens were in coops on the farm. It was an active dairy and egg operation. Soon, Eisenhower discovered that many of his cows had brucellosis and needed to be put down. The crop fields needed improvement as well. Eisenhower implemented the latest agricultural techniques, such as crop rotation, strip cropping, contour plowing, adding fertilizer and manure, and installing grass waterways to conserve topsoil. The results were improved crop yields. (Above, ENHS2878, Henry Blatner; below, ENHS2876, LS.)

In December 1950, Pres. Harry Truman asked Eisenhower to become the first commander of SHAPE (Supreme Headquarters, Allied Powers, Europe) for the North Atlantic Treaty Organization, or NATO. He was the unanimous choice of the 12 original alliance members. Eisenhower was, by all accounts, a tonic for the Western Alliance. Here, Ike leans on a globe at SHAPE while James Dunn, the US ambassador to France, looks on. (ENHS2366, PRC.)

Eisenhower wasted no time transitioning to his new responsibilities at NATO. Following a brief trip to meet colleagues and survey circumstances on the ground, Ike returned to report to the president, who met him at Washington National Airport on January 31, 1951, before a large contingent of media. (HSTL73-3497, NPS, Abbie Rowe.)

To supervise farm operations while he was abroad as supreme commander of SHAPE and then as a presidential candidate traversing the country, Eisenhower recruited his friend retired general Arthur Nevins, brother of the noted historian Allan Nevins. Nevins and Eisenhower pose in a pasture on the day of a picnic hosted for Pennsylvania delegates to the Republican National Convention, June 13, 1952. (ENHS2220, LS14670-14.)

Eisenhower could not improve his farm property without the assistance of General Nevins and a small band of dedicated workers, among them Ivan Feaster—here shown on an Allis-Chalmers tractor with manure spreader in late January 1953, only days after his employer was sworn in as the 34th president of the United States. (ENHS2879, LS15556-2.)

Winning the Republican nomination for president was job one—and no simple task—as Eisenhower returned from Europe in June 1952. After making his first campaign speech in Abilene, Kansas, Ike returned to Gettysburg to meet with Republican delegates from Pennsylvania, whose allegiance lay in the balance between Ike and Sen. Robert Taft of Ohio. In the above photograph, Ike stands in front of his farmhouse and shares his views on current issues with the media and fellow Republicans attending the picnic on June 13, 1952. In the photograph at right, he is flanked by Gov. John Fine (still on the fence between Ike and Senator Taft) on his left and US senator James Duff of Pennsylvania (an early Eisenhower backer) on his right. (Above, ENHS2207, LS14670-7; right, ENHS2208, Paul Roy.)

Ike flashes his trademark grin in between bites of fried chicken at the Republican picnic at the farm on June 13, 1952. Milk from the Eisenhower dairy cows was also served to attendees. Evidently, the delegates liked the milk and chicken and they liked Ike; a strong majority of the Pennsylvania delegation backed the general at the Republican convention in Chicago. (ENHS2223, LS14670-6.)

Ensconced in the living room of his new home, Eisenhower reads the local paper's account of his candidacy, flanked by *Gettysburg Times* editor Paul Roy, left, and publisher Henry Scharf. Roy's allegiance to Ike was not in doubt. (ENHS2216, LS14670-1.)

Eisenhower's triumph in Chicago was not a done deal until the close of the first ballot, when Minnesota delegates pledged to former governor Harold Stassen gained recognition from the convention chair and bolted to Eisenhower, putting him over the top. Ike chose 39-year-old California senator Richard M. Nixon as his running mate, bringing both youth and geographical balance to the ticket. Here, the two men clasp hands at the GOP convention in Chicago in a show of unity before commencing a grueling fall campaign. (AP329627941278.)

Neither Ike nor Mamie relished the idea of barnstorming through the country to earn votes, but they were game for it and proved adept campaigners. Ike later claimed that the highlights of his many whistle-stops came at the close of his remarks when he would invite the boisterous crowds to greet "my Mamie" as she came to the platform and waved. Here, the Eisenhowers make an unplanned appearance—in their pajamas, no less—in Salisbury, North Carolina, on September 26, 1952. (EL71-328-1, Republican National Committee.)

Maintaining a modest lead over Democrat Adlai Stevenson of Illinois, Eisenhower broke the campaign open on October 27 in Detroit, with a promise to "go to Korea." Voters believed that the hero of D-day could solve whatever ailed the US military effort in Korea. They rewarded the Eisenhower/Nixon ticket with a landslide victory. This photograph captures Ike in a military jeep with Gen. Mark Clark and others during a visit to the Korean front on December 7, 1952. On July 27, 1953, the Eisenhower administration concluded the Korean War armistice. (EL65-107, USA.)

Four

THE GETTYSBURG FARM
BECOMES A HOME

The presidency is a pressure cooker. At age 62 when he took the oath of office, Dwight Eisenhower needed to find ways to ease up and relieve stress. Regular golf outings were a great stress reducer for the president. He even practiced his game on the White House South Lawn, including putting on a US Golf Association–donated green. Camp David offered the opportunity to let his hair down and meet informally with government officials and foreign visitors. But perhaps most important for Ike and Mamie was the use of their Gettysburg home—renovations completed by the spring of 1955—as a retreat from the everyday pressures of Washington life.

Eisenhower often said he wanted to leave a piece of ground better than he found it. That was manifestly the case with the family home, which underwent a stem-to-stern overhaul. For the Eisenhowers, their Gettysburg address was first and foremost a family place, its decor unpretentious and quintessentially in keeping with the Midcentury Modern motifs popular at the time. A glassed-in porch overlooking the eastern portion of the Eisenhower property was an afterthought in the house construction, but without doubt it became the Eisenhowers' favorite room. There, they entertained friends for bridge, played Scrabble, watched television, and ate some of their meals. Ike used the porch for painting, at which he grew increasingly adept during the White House years.

Improvements to the farm also gave Eisenhower an outlet. He consulted with the Soil Conservation Service and the Pennsylvania State University County Extension agent about the best ways to improve his farm. Recommendations on the latest agricultural techniques like contour plowing, crop rotation, and strip cropping were all implemented to improve productivity. The suggestion that some fields were best used as pasture tied in with Eisenhower's interest in raising registered Angus cattle. Success in improving the breed was measured by winning ribbons at cattle shows. A cattle partnership with several friends and the joint hiring of a professional herdsman allowed Eisenhower's small Angus herd to grow in size and quality, winning over 600 ribbons and banners in the next 10 years.

The Eisenhower farm was not merely a retreat. The Eisenhowers threw occasional picnics for Republican activists and White House staff, including one in 1959 that included African American White House domestic staffers and their significant others—probably the first such social event hosted by an American president.

On January 20, 1953, Eisenhower took the oath of office as the nation's 34th president—the first Republican president since Herbert Hoover. Chief Justice Fred Vinson, flanked by outgoing president Harry S. Truman, administered the oath. A solemn looking Richard M. Nixon, Eisenhower's newly inaugurated vice president, looks on. (ENHS1595, NPS.)

After lunch, the inaugural parade began. It lasted for two and a half hours and was the most elaborate to date. An estimated one million people attended the parade, 60,000 of them in grandstand seating. This photograph captures Ike and Mamie entering the White House for the first time, on the evening of January 20. (NARA111-SC-413247.)

Eisenhower was the last president to use the cabinet as a deliberative body. This July 29, 1955, photograph includes cabinet members and other key aides. Note one woman at the table: Oveta Culp Hobby, who served briefly as secretary of the newly created Department of Health, Education, and Welfare. Attendees from left to right include Wilton Persons, Henry Cabot Lodge, Douglas McKay, George Humphrey, Richard Nixon, Herbert Brownell, Sinclair Weeks, Oveta Culp Hobby, Philip Young, Rowland Hughes, Arthur Flemming, Maxwell Rabb, James Mitchell, Arthur Summerfield, John Foster Dulles, President Eisenhower, Charles Wilson, Ezra Taft Benson, Harold Stassen, and Sherman Adams. (EL72-1466-1, NPS, Abbie Rowe.)

Once the Eisenhowers settled into the White House, Mamie insisted that it was time to begin work on their Gettysburg home. By the autumn of 1953, architectural plans were drawn and dismantling of the old house began. The picture above, taken on November 17, 1953, shows removal of bricks on the north end of the house, exposing logs that likely dated to 1740 when the property was first settled. The logs had rotted, and the builder recommended tearing the entire structure down and starting from scratch. Mamie was determined to save as much of the original house as possible. The photograph below, taken on January 26, 1954, shows the solid brick addition that was built in the mid-19th century. It was salvaged, as was the bake oven from the summer kitchen. (Above, AP199723622391; below, ENHS1103, PRC.)

As demolition continued, the Eisenhowers determined to save the windmill that had provided water to the original farmhouse. Though it was no longer needed to pump water as the Eisenhowers ran a new water line to the property, they liked the look of the windmill on the farm. The site was now ready for constructing a substantially new dwelling around the few salvaged parts of the old structure. (ENHS1100, PRC.)

In the spring of 1954, construction of the redesigned Eisenhower home began in earnest. This photograph provides a view of brickmasons at work on the northwest corner of the new structure, with the outline of the Eisenhowers' living room, front hall, and dining room visible. (ENHS2791, GT.)

With the exterior masonry work complete and the slate roof well under way, on August 13, 1954, Mamie was ready to show her house to the cabinet wives who arrived by car for the outing. To the left of the tree is the new construction, which housed the living room, entrance hall, and dining room. Behind the tree is the salvaged brick section, which became the butler's pantry and kitchen. The stone addition connected the salvaged section to the bake oven and became Ike's den. (ENHS2799, NPS, Abbie Rowe.)

On October 4, 1954, Butts Tree Movers of Cairo, New York, planted a white pine tree next to the bake oven on the south side of the house. This tree and five others were a gift from Nelson A. Rockefeller, then serving as special assistant to the president. White pines were Eisenhower's favorite tree. (ENHS1124.)

These two images depict the Eisenhower home, front and rear, shortly after renovations were completed. The decision to paint the brick white had been implemented likely because of the difference between texture and color of the old and new brick. The barn color was also changed from red to a gray-green, personally mixed by Eisenhower and approved by Mamie. On the east side or rear of the house, elaborate landscaping and flower beds were installed. During Ike's retirement, the round flower beds were removed to simplify grounds maintenance. The putting green, a gift of the Professional Golfers Association, was installed on the east side of the house, with Eisenhower explaining, "Mrs. Ike says that the green simply must be some place where she can sit on the porch and watch us practice." (Above, ENHS1135; below, ENHS1136.)

With friend George Allen and Texan Billy Byars, Eisenhower began acquiring his small herd of registered Angus cattle to be raised on their farms. They hired Robert Hartley, a talented herdsman and Pennsylvania State University graduate, to come to Gettysburg and supervise the cattle breeding program. In the above photograph, taken on December 13, 1954, Ike walks through the corral with cattle behind him. In the photograph below, taken on August 9, 1955, Ike stands with his hand on a Holstein heifer during a presentation by Montgomery County, Maryland, 4-H members Thomas King and Roberta Messer. Later, Holstein cows were used as nurse cows for the Angus show herd. As his herd grew, Eisenhower's cattle were shown at competitions under his partners' names so judges would not know they belonged to the president. (Above, EL72-1132-6, the Queens Borough Public Library, Archives, *New York Herald-Tribune* photograph Morgue Collection; below, EL72-1483-5.)

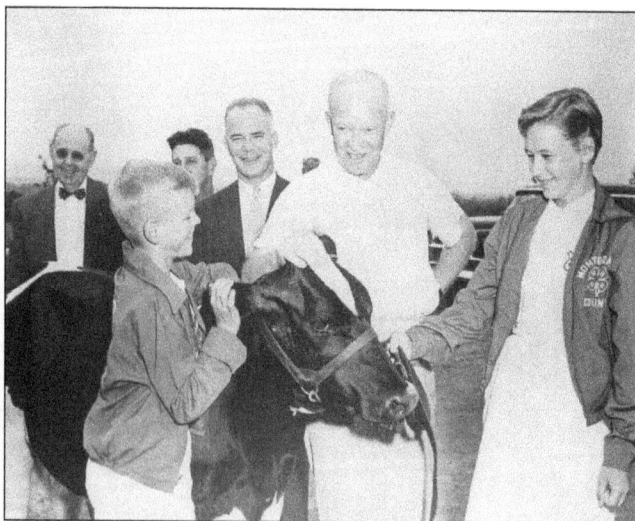

Landscape enhancements were integral to the Eisenhower dwelling in Gettysburg. In late 1955, Norway spruce trees, gifts of each state's Republican committee, were planted along the drive from Millerstown Road to the house. (EL67-108-2, USN.)

From the start, the Eisenhowers planned to have roses at their home. This east bed of assorted hybrid tea roses brightened the backyard on July 25, 1956. Landscaper Walter West, a chief petty officer assigned to the presidential retreat, Camp David, remembers planting President Lincoln, Charlotte Armstrong, White Radiance, Peace, Talisman, and Hoover cultivars. The General Eisenhower rose was a gift from Chancellor Konrad Adenauer of West Germany. Fifty red General Eisenhower roses were planted in the nearby North Rose Garden. (ENHS2931, USN.)

To mark their 39th wedding anniversary in July 1955 at their Gettysburg farm, the Eisenhowers threw a picnic for the White House staff. At one point during the event, they took a brief respite from greeting guests to pose for a photograph. Standing in front of their home, as Eisenhower leans against his Crosley Runabout, Mamie's attention is turned, admiringly, to her husband. (EL67-99-2, USN.)

Five

PRESIDENTIAL BUSINESS
AT THE FARM

Mamie Eisenhower had a rule that when Ike entered the family quarters at the White House or walked through the front door of their home in Gettysburg, work was to be left behind. Her intention was good as she knew that her husband needed a break from the burdens of the presidency. By and large, Ike obliged, but sometimes presidential business crept into their home. At the White House, that might mean an evening meeting with Secretary of State John Foster Dulles in the family quarters. At Gettysburg during vacation periods, legislation was signed, the State of the Union address edited, work on the federal budget ensued, and plans for welcoming foreign leaders or traveling overseas were made. At the farm, Eisenhower kept tabs on national security matters, as well as the flow of congressional legislation. John Eisenhower recalled that weekends at the farm always included a 45-minute briefing on world events so the president was up-to-date and ready to act on any new problem, if needed.

In September 1955, President Eisenhower suffered a heart attack while they were visiting Mamie's mother in Denver, Colorado. When he left the hospital in November 1955, the Gettysburg farm took on added significance as it became the temporary White House. Ike wrote: "I was glad to go to Gettysburg to recover, not only because of the restful atmosphere there, but because I felt that I could do my necessary work as readily at the farm as I could at the White House." Eisenhower spent the next 36 days running the country from Gettysburg. Business was conducted at the farmhouse and also at an office set up in the Gettysburg Post Office, the federal building in town. Eisenhower made an effort to go to this temporary office every day so that the press would photograph him going to and from work, thus ensuring the American people that their president was well and on the job.

Concerns about Eisenhower's health led to the question of whether he would run for a second term as president. As he recovered, Ike decided that his work was not done. The farm served as backdrop for a campaign event prior to the 1956 election. After reelection, Eisenhower continued to use the farm to conduct presidential business. From the completion of house renovations in 1955 until he left office in 1961, Eisenhower spent 365 full or partial days at his farm.

During Eisenhower's two terms in office, television came to dominate the interface between the president and the American people. Prodded by press secretary James Hagerty, Ike began holding regular, nationally televised press conferences. He also periodically addressed the American people on pressing issues, notably civil rights and the Cold War. Here, he is captured as he prepared to make an address late in his presidency, surrounded by microphone, drapes, flag, and the presidential seal. (EL70-654, NPS.)

Contrary to what one might expect when it comes to presidential perquisites, the office at the Eisenhowers' home was snug and unpretentious. In fact, Eisenhower said he liked a small office where he could focus his energies. In these two photographs, the president is in the process of signing formal documents, using a fountain pen, no less! During his summer vacation, Eisenhower signed about 40 pieces of legislation. White House counsel Gerald Warren reviews one document while confidential secretary Ann Whitman hands him the next one to sign on August 9, 1955. (Above, EL72-1482-2, NPS; below, EL72-1482-1, NPS.)

Eisenhower and motorcades went together like love and marriage. In this instance, returning to Gettysburg in November 1955, following his heart attack, Ike drew a large and enthusiastic crowd. Note the Secret Service agents beside the car. Behind him in this photograph stands the David Wills House, where Abraham Lincoln spent the night of November 18, 1863, before delivering his immortal address. (ENHS2255, GT, Paul Roy.)

In wake of his heart attack, Eisenhower was welcomed home on November 14, 1955, with considerable fanfare by Gettysburg citizens. Here, Ike waves to the crowd, Mamie at his side, just prior to brief remarks by Gettysburg mayor William G. Weaver, smiling, center. (ENHS2000, Paul Roy.)

During his 36-day heart attack convalescence in Gettysburg, Ike had three places available to him for conducting business: his farm home and office, Glatfelter Hall on the Gettysburg College campus where television and radio broadcasts were made, and this one in the Gettysburg Post Office on Baltimore Street. This photograph shows the office shortly after Ike arrived in Gettysburg from Fitzsimmons Army Hospital in Denver, Colorado. (ENHS1453, Paul Roy.)

Most members of the Eisenhower cabinet made it to Pennsylvania at least once during the Gettysburg sojourn. Here, Eisenhower confers with Secretary of State John Foster Dulles in the president's office at the post office on November 18, 1955. (AP168707788826.)

Barely a week after returning to Gettysburg, Eisenhower filmed an address for a White House conference on education. Here, he departs Glatfelter Hall on the college campus, where he delivered his remarks on November 23, 1955. Television adviser Robert Montgomery trails him. On December 18, Ike was back at the college to deliver his "Christmas Message to the Nation" and, by remote control, turn on the Christmas tree lights in Washington, DC. (ENHS1330, GT.)

For convenience, meetings with the cabinet during the convalescence sometimes took place at the presidential retreat, Camp David, in Maryland, less than 20 miles south of Gettysburg. At this November 22, 1955, meeting, Ike leans towards Secretary of State John Foster Dulles. Secretary of Agriculture Ezra Taft Benson smiles at the president, as Secretary of Defense Charles Wilson (turned away from camera) converses with other cabinet members. (ENHS3468, PRC.)

The White House Press Corps always follows the president, and it always needs space to conduct its business. To meet this need, Hotel Gettysburg owner Henry Scharf converted the gymnasium adjacent to his business into a White House pressroom, where daily briefings were part of the regimen and occasional headline news would break. (ENHS3342, GT.)

As new Gettysburg residents, the Eisenhowers intended to do their civic duty and register to vote—Republican, of course. On February 3, 1956, Ike and Mamie showed their newly minted voter cards in the Adams County Courthouse, as the registrar and other local officials look on. (ENHS2008, GT, Paul Roy.)

On September 12, 1956, to launch his reelection campaign, Ike hosted a rally/picnic at the farm for 500 Republican Party workers and delegates. Note the tents set up a good distance from Ike's cherished putting green. Some of the young women who "liked Ike" showed their enthusiasm for the candidate by dressing for the occasion and carrying Ike parasols, clearly catching the president's admiring eye. (Above, AP368416095615; below, ENHS2011, PRC.)

At the campaign kickoff event, Mamie wore her own distinctive dress, made from a special Eisenhower toile designed by Elisabeth Draper and depicting many of the places the Eisenhowers had lived. President Eisenhower fanned the fabric to give Vice Pres. Richard Nixon and his wife, Pat, a better chance to admire it. At the close of the day, Ike spoke to the assembled crowd, reminding them that the election would be a referendum on his administration and encouraging those attending to get the word out about peace and prosperity as the Republicans' calling card. As one pundit put it, "Everything is booming except the guns." (Above, EL72-1868-15; below, ENHS2010, GT, Paul Roy.)

Although the president conducted the majority of serious business in the White House, meetings relating to the budget or the State of the Union address occasionally were held in Gettysburg. On New Year's Eve, December 1957, Ike met with three of his advisers to discuss the coming year's budget. From left to right are Eisenhower, budget director Percival Brundage, science adviser James R. Killian, and deputy budget director Maurice Stans. (ENHS2304, GT, Paul Roy.)

In 1959, Ike took advantage of Henry Scharf's hospitality and set up his summer vacation office in the Hotel Gettysburg, in what had been the Scharfs' private apartment. John Eisenhower unrolls a large document for the president to review on August 13, 1959. A topic that was likely discussed during this working vacation was the upcoming visit by Soviet premier Nikita Khrushchev. (ENHS1239, PRC.)

Six

DAILY LIFE AT THE FARM

With the exceptions of Bill Clinton and Barack Obama, every president has had an identifiable home base during the White House years, a site regularly used for recreation and business alike. At John Adams's homestead in Braintree, Massachusetts, the second president liked nothing better than to shovel his manure pile. Thomas Jefferson had Monticello; Abraham Lincoln the Soldiers' Home outside of Washington, DC; and Franklin Roosevelt was keen to spend time at his ancestral home in Hyde Park.

For Dwight Eisenhower, Gettysburg was an ideal second home during the White House years. Its proximity to Washington (and Camp David, for that matter), its connection to the Civil War, and its rustic charm, all made the Gettysburg farm "right" for Ike and Mamie Eisenhower. By all evidence, they enjoyed it immensely, right down to Ike's many golf outings at the Gettysburg Country Club and Mamie's shopping at local stores. Both Eisenhowers intended to become full participants in the life of the community they called home.

How they worshiped and where they voted exemplify this plan. The Eisenhowers regularly attended services at the Gettysburg Presbyterian Church on Baltimore Street. Now registered in Pennsylvania, Ike flew to Gettysburg by helicopter to vote in the 1958 midterm election. Eisenhower not only did some business on the Gettysburg College campus, but in 1959 he made a major address about world peace there.

The focal point of the Eisenhowers' Gettysburg life in the 1950s, however, was the farmstead, where holidays and other special occasions were marked and where the Eisenhower grandchildren had the opportunity to ride horses and, in grandson David's case, learn the rudiments of golf under the attentive eye of his granddad. Mamie maintained a prodigious correspondence during her sojourns in Gettysburg. For his part, the president found a way of balancing his official duties with recreating in various respects: shooting skeet, playing bridge, painting, overseeing his show cattle operation, reading history, and perfecting his golf game. All told, Gettysburg was a healthy place for the Eisenhowers.

Ike and Mamie marked their 40th wedding anniversary on July 1, 1956, more quietly than the previous year. Here, they pose on the terrace on the east side of the house, Mamie again wearing her Eisenhower toile dress, Ike dressed in business casual. They look very happy. (ENHS3577, USN.)

Nothing gave the president and first lady more pleasure than spending time with son John and his family. In August 1954, Ike and Mamie pose on the patio of the presidential retreat Camp David with John; his wife, Barbara; and their three children. Ike holds Susan (born December 31, 1951), Mamie holds David (born March 31, 1948), and Anne (born May 30, 1949) stands with her father. Mary Jean was born the following year on December 21, 1955. (EL67-83-63, USN.)

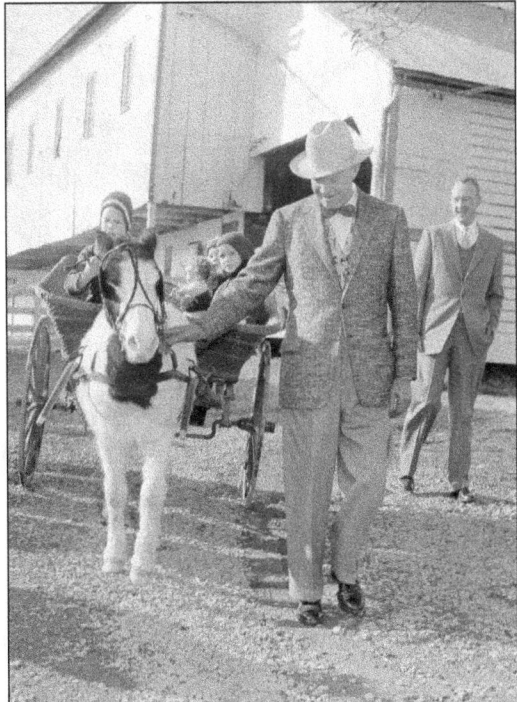

During Thanksgiving 1955, Ike led the grandkids on a pony cart ride, with their dad, John, looking on. Grandson David remembered "suiting up" for the picture-taking session. He recollected, "Picture-taking sessions were all very formal. . . . It was very time-consuming and usually uncomfortable because we wore a lot of wool back then and I'm faintly allergic to wool. However, we didn't question it of course." (AP306548549287.)

The specially designed Crosley golf cart for ready navigation on the farm came in handy for a media photo opportunity on September 16, 1956. Photographers captured Ike at the wheel with grandson David in front, while Mamie held granddaughters Anne and Susan in the backseat. The east side of the barn next to the Eisenhower residence is in the background. (EL72-1868-30, NPS.)

Given the president's golf addiction, it was inevitable he would encourage grandson David to take up the sport at a tender age. In this photograph, Eisenhower and his son John tutor David on his putting on the green at Camp David, August 1, 1954. (EL67-83, USN.)

Hoisting his cap and carrying a starter set of clubs, David waves to cameramen at the Gettysburg Country Club on May 6, 1956, as his granddad, quite pleased with the tableau, looks on. (ENHS1572, GT.)

Eisenhower was a serious golfer and, contrary to some reports, quite adept. His most regular partners at the Gettysburg Country Club included his son John, his caddie Arthur "Art" Kennell, and Gen. Arthur Nevins, the latter pictured here riding with Ike on May 21, 1960—three weeks after the U-2 incident largely smashed Ike's dreams of a lasting détente with the Soviet Union. Note the caddies behind them, hustling to keep up. (ENHS1401, GT.)

67

Eisenhower's goal for his farm was to leave it better than he found it. He improved the soil using sound agricultural principles, such as crop rotation, strip cropping, and the application of fertilizer and manure, to make the land as productive as possible. He also wanted to improve the Angus cattle breed. To assist him in the goal, the Eisenhower farms partnership hired Robert Hartley as herdsman. Hartley's experience with breeding and showing cattle netted the Eisenhower cattle herd many ribbons from 1957 to 1966. Here, Hartley poses with Pennsylvania Farm Show champion bull Keystone Bardoliermere E-2 in the yard north of the show barn in January 1962. (ENHS1445, GT, Robert Hartley Collection.)

The Eisenhowers were often offered, and accepted, gifts for the farm and home from admirers. In one case, it was a Cockshutt Blackhawk tractor, loaded with gadgets, donated in November 1955 by an association of Pennsylvania, Ohio, and Indiana farmers. Ivan Feaster stands behind the president's left shoulder. In another instance, Ike stands with a Black Angus heifer and calf donated by the Brandywine Angus Breeders Association on June 3, 1955. Farm manager Arthur Nevins, far left, observes the scene. Ike looks happier than the heifer. (Above, AP164306953169; right, EL72-1398-3, NPS.)

When in Gettysburg, the Eisenhowers often attended services at the Presbyterian church on Baltimore Street—noticeably building attendance there. In May 1956, Ike and Mamie made an exception to their routine by attending Sunday services at Christ Chapel on the Gettysburg College campus. Here, Ike departs from the chapel accompanied by former Gettysburg College president Henry W.A. Hanson, as students and local citizens greet them. (ENHS1337, GT.)

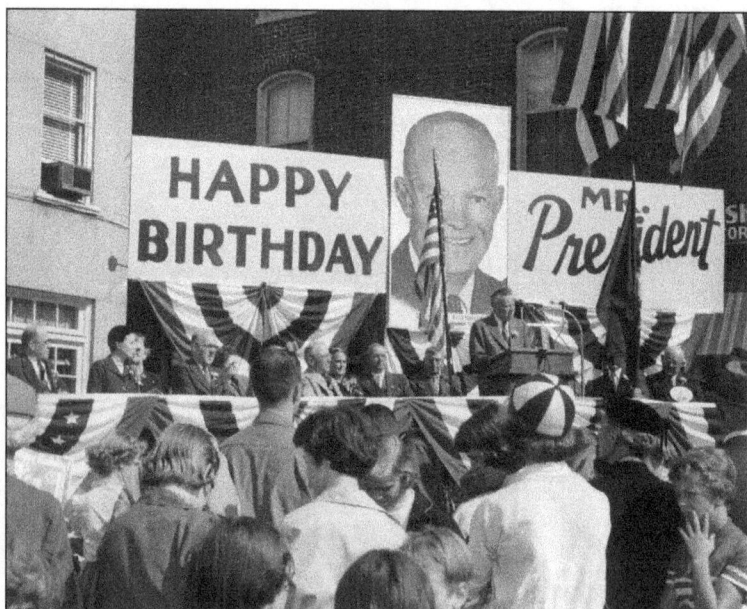

Ever ready to show their pride in their favorite son, Gettysburg residents sponsored a birthday celebration for Ike in Lincoln Square, directly in front of the Hotel Gettysburg, in October 1956. Eisenhower was not present, except in spirit. (ENHS1494, ACHS, ZS.)

Gettysburg Times photographer Paul Roy captured Mamie (flanked by son John and daughter-in-law Barbara) for an Easter portrait in 1958. The setting was the back porch of the Eisenhower home. The children are, from left to right, David, Susan, Anne, and Mary Jean. (EL65-942-1, BEC, Paul Roy.)

In 1957, John and Barbara Eisenhower purchased the renovated Pitzer schoolhouse adjacent to the Eisenhower farm property. They moved to Gettysburg in 1959. John, on the White House staff, spent the week in Washington and came home on weekends. This move allowed Barbara and the children to fully integrate into the Gettysburg community. This photograph shows Barbara (back to camera) chatting with a friend, while David rides his bike. (ENHS1141, BEC.)

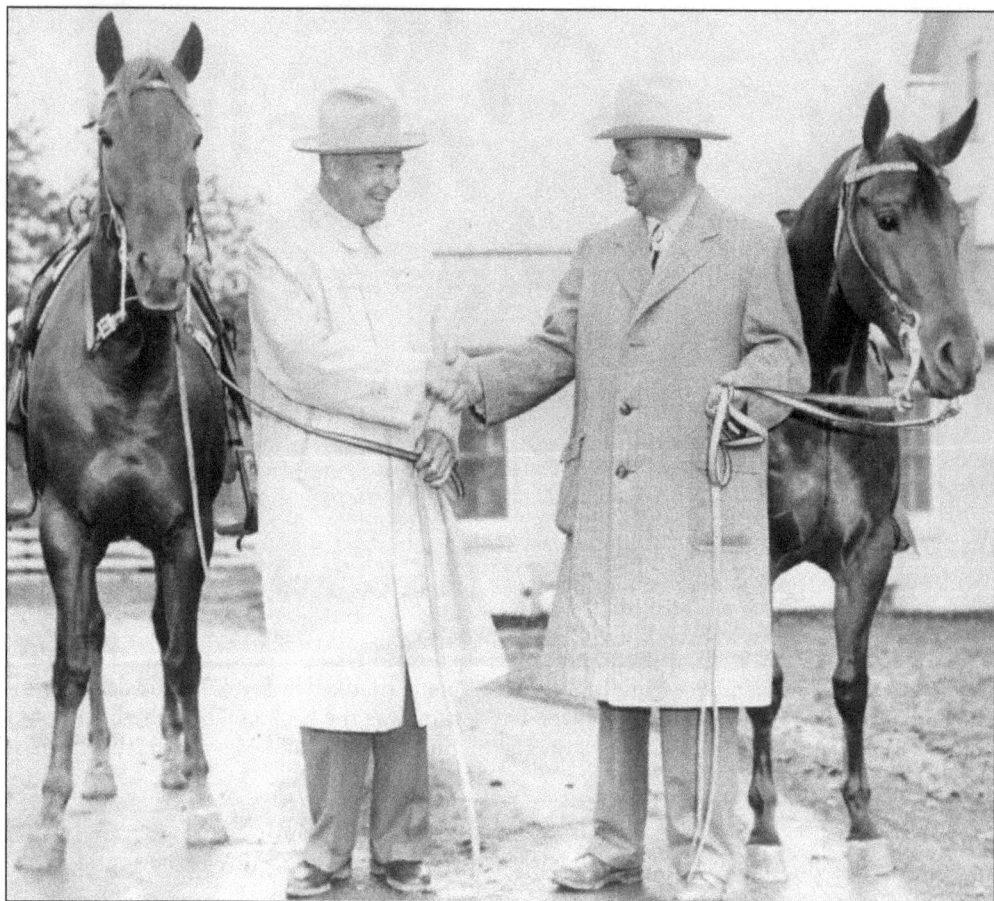

Eisenhower seems especially enthusiastic accepting two horses from the American Quarter Horse Association on a rainy June 2, 1956. Doodle De Do's reins are held by Ike, while Lester Goodson of the association holds the reins for Sporty Miss. As the photograph at left shows, David, peeking under the horse's neck, rode Doodle De Do, while Susan was given instruction on riding Sporty Miss, November 1957. The John Eisenhower home is visible in the distance. (Above, ENHS2516, PRC; left, ENHS1221, GT.)

One of the distinctive elements of the Eisenhower home was its glass-enclosed porch, depicted here in July 1955, shortly after the completion of house renovations. In the foreground are the terrace, flagstone walk, and Frisco Bell featuring the presidential seal, a gift from Clark Hungerford, the president of the Frisco Railroad. The bell was originally used on a locomotive operated by the St. Louis-San Francisco Railway Company. The scene of bridge games, television watching, Ike's oil painting, family gatherings, and Scrabble contests, the porch was the Eisenhowers' favorite room. (EL71-948-34.)

Eisenhower flew by helicopter to Gettysburg in order to cast his vote in the midterm elections on November 4, 1958. Here, he has just disembarked from an Army craft and is greeting Earl Pitzer, the Adams County Republican chairman. Joining the president are John and Barbara Eisenhower, John and Delores Moaney, and an unidentified man at far left. Mamie, who disliked flying, came by car from Washington to vote. (ENHS2317, GT.)

John Moaney, pictured here with Eisenhower in the early 1960s, began his service as one of General Eisenhower's orderlies during World War II. After the war, Moaney asked to stay on with the general. He was devoted to Ike and served as an honorary pallbearer at Eisenhower's funeral in March 1969. (ENHS2521, LS33000-1.)

Mamie greets staff members and their families at a picnic on June 6, 1959. Both the office and domestic staff of the White House were invited. Among the guests that day was E. Frederic Morrow, the first African American to serve in an executive capacity in any White House. Morrow is second from left speaking to an unidentified woman, likely his wife. Guests were gathered near the rose garden, east of the main house. (Above, ENHS2333, MJMC; below, ENHS2328, MJMC.)

Eisenhower had promised Gettysburg College president Willard S. Paul that he would speak at Gettysburg College at some point during his presidency. On April 4, 1959, Eisenhower made good on his promise, delivering a convocation speech focused on prospects for world peace. (GCSC, GEI_9553, ACHS, LS.)

To promote world peace, Eisenhower invited Soviet premier Nikita Khrushchev to visit the United States. An impromptu visit to the president's farm resulted in reduced Cold War tensions, but eight months later, a U-2 reconnaissance plane was shot down over the Soviet Union. On May 25, 1960, Ike spoke from the Oval Office about the U-2 incident and Khrushchev's decision to abort the Paris summit meeting designed to foster détente. Eisenhower's son John looks on. (EL72-3441-6, NPS, Abbie Rowe.)

Seven

DIGNITARIES VISIT THE FARM

With the completed renovations to the farmhouse and barns, President Eisenhower began hosting world leaders at the farm. He believed in personal diplomacy, world leaders meeting face-to-face. Eisenhower said that talking in a relaxed atmosphere without all the advisers present allowed him to "take the measure of the man."

Visits always included a tour of the Eisenhower farm cattle barns with Eisenhower knowledgeably explaining various aspects of raising registered Angus show cattle. Herdsman Bob Hartley was usually on hand to answer any in-depth questions. After the farm tour, guests were invited to sit on the enclosed porch of the house for some refreshment and conversation.

Prime Minister Jawaharlal Nehru from India was the first world leader to visit, in December 1956. He and Eisenhower conducted 14 hours of private talks that weekend, giving Eisenhower a valuable perspective on the Cold War from a neutral country's vantage. Others followed, including Konrad Adenauer of West Germany, Prime Minister Harold Macmillan of Great Britain, Pres. Charles de Gaulle of France, and Premier Nikita Khrushchev of the Soviet Union. Pres. Adolfo Lopez Mateos of Mexico and Pres. Alberto Lleras Camargo of Colombia were also Eisenhower's guests.

As John Eisenhower remembered, "When my father was president, he developed the habit of bringing visiting world leaders to the farm. Such informality, he reasoned, would make them feel at home. Visiting dignitaries soon got the word of such favored treatment, so everybody had to be brought to the farm, so they would receive what everybody else had!"

Longtime military associates also visited. British field marshal Bernard Montgomery spent the weekend at the farm and toured the battlefield with Eisenhower in May 1957. Former prime minister Winston Churchill visited in May 1959. Since he had had a stroke, Churchill toured the cattle barns in the Crosley Runabout and by golf cart. Then, Eisenhower also took him on a helicopter tour of the battlefield before they headed back to Washington.

Even in retirement, Eisenhower continued to receive distinguished visitors at his farm. Former vice president Richard Nixon, presidential candidate Barry Goldwater, and California gubernatorial candidate Ronald Reagan came to consult him. And world leaders continued to visit. In the 1960s, Pres. Ayub Khan of Pakistan, Vice Pres. Chen Cheng of the Republic of China (Taiwan), King Zahir and Queen Homaira of Afghanistan, Philippine president Ferdinand Marcos, and the king of Nepal visited, reciprocating Eisenhower's visits to their countries during his world tours in December 1959 and June 1960.

A smiling President Eisenhower points to his cattle in the pasture at Farm 2 as Indian prime minister Jawaharlal Nehru enjoys the tour on December 17, 1956. Between the two stands farm manager Arthur Nevins as members of the press and Secret Service agents look on. (ENHS2463, ANC.)

Sir Winston Churchill and Eisenhower return from a tour of the cattle barns in the Crosley Runabout on May 6, 1959. Secret Service agents drive and stand on the specially designed running board at the rear of the Crosley. Churchill's 75-minute visit at the farm concluded with a helicopter tour of the battlefield. (EL72-3078-7, NPS.)

Eisenhower and British field marshal Montgomery stand on the summit of Little Round Top discussing the Battle of Gettysburg while press secretary Jim Hagerty looks on. Houck's Ridge and Crawford Avenue are visible behind them. They toured the battlefield with the White House Press Corps in tow. (EL72-2233-4, NPS.)

Eisenhower and Montgomery point to features during the Electric Map program in the Gettysburg National Museum on May 12, 1957. As John Eisenhower remembered later, "At the Virginia Memorial they looked across the field (of Pickett's Charge) and Monty said, 'Monstrous, monstrous.' He turned to Dad and said, 'What would you do to me if I did that?' By this time, I think the old man's blood pressure was way up and he said, 'I'd a sacked you!' Well, . . . the newspapers interpreted it to mean that 'Eisenhower would have sacked General Lee.' This was terrible. So then they had to make a big point of Dad's having a picture of General Lee on the wall of his office at the White House." (ENHS2443, LS22790-10.)

Eisenhower and West German chancellor Konrad Adenauer stand at a wire fence along the farm lane as Ike points out an Angus cow, yearling, and calf on May 26, 1957. (EL72-2255-7, NPS, Abbie Rowe.)

Ike and Adenauer admire the farm's herd bull Ankonian 3551 under the forebay of the bank barn on Farm 2 as the translator talks to Adenauer. According to John Eisenhower, Adenauer was not a fan of artificial insemination, preferring the natural method instead. (EL72-2255-13, GT.)

Eisenhower and Soviet premier Nikita Khrushchev pose outside of Aspen Lodge at the presidential retreat Camp David. When talks on the Berlin Ultimatum bogged down, Ike flew Khrushchev to the farm for a change of scenery. The premier toured the cattle barns and met the Eisenhower grandchildren on the porch. He even extended an invitation to John, Barbara, and the grandchildren to visit the Soviet Union the following spring. Then, both men returned to Camp David and made progress on the Berlin issue. (EL67-309-8, USN, Knudsen.)

Eisenhower and Pres. Adolfo López Mateos, followed by military aides, arrive at the farm on October 10, 1959. Improved relations resulted in the construction of a radar tracking station in Mexico, essential for NASA's Project Mercury. During the visit, López Mateos watched an equestrian performance by granddaughter Susan Eisenhower. (EL67-314-2, USN, Knudsen.)

Pres. Alberto Lleras Camargo of Colombia visited Camp David for talks with Eisenhower on April 7, 1960. That evening, they arrived at the farm for a 45-minute tour of the show barn and the nearby home of John Eisenhower. (ENHS2470, PRC.)

Eisenhower and French president Charles de Gaulle tour the Gettysburg battlefield, stopping to examine the Whitworth cannon at Schultz Woods along West Confederate Avenue on April 24, 1960. Commander Flohic, interpreter, stands at left. Later, Eisenhower noted that de Gaulle was an excellent student of the battle. (AP921713423178.)

As they tour the show barn, de Gaulle admires the prize ribbons won by Eisenhower's cattle. With the Paris summit meeting between the United States, the Soviet Union, France, and Great Britain to discuss Berlin only three weeks away, that topic likely came up during the French president's visit. (ENHS1400A, BEC.)

Eisenhower, giving a V sign for "victory," and former vice president Richard Nixon pose at the front door of the house on August 28, 1961. This was Nixon's first visit back to the farm since leaving office. The two had dinner together. (ENHS1407, GT, Paul Roy.)

New York governor Nelson Rockefeller meets with Eisenhower at his office on the campus of Gettysburg College on July 11, 1961. Many people met with Eisenhower at his Gettysburg College office; only a few of them were also invited to the farm. (ENHS1406, PRC.)

Eisenhower meets with fellow Republicans in his Gettysburg College office on May 1, 1961. From left to right are (sitting) Sen. Everett Dirksen, Eisenhower, and Rep. Charles Halleck; (standing) Charles Hoeven, Republican Conference chairman; Thurston Morton, Republican National Committee chairman; John Byrnes; Sen. Leverett Saltonstall; Leslie Arends, House whip; Clarence Brown; and Thomas Kuchel, Senate whip. (ENHS1412, PRC.)

Eisenhower and Civil War historian Bruce Catton examine the High Water Mark Monument at Gettysburg National Military Park in 1962. Catton joined Eisenhower in filming the television show *Lincoln: Commander in Chief.* During the interview, Eisenhower showed the portrait of President Lincoln he painted. (EL63-521-2.)

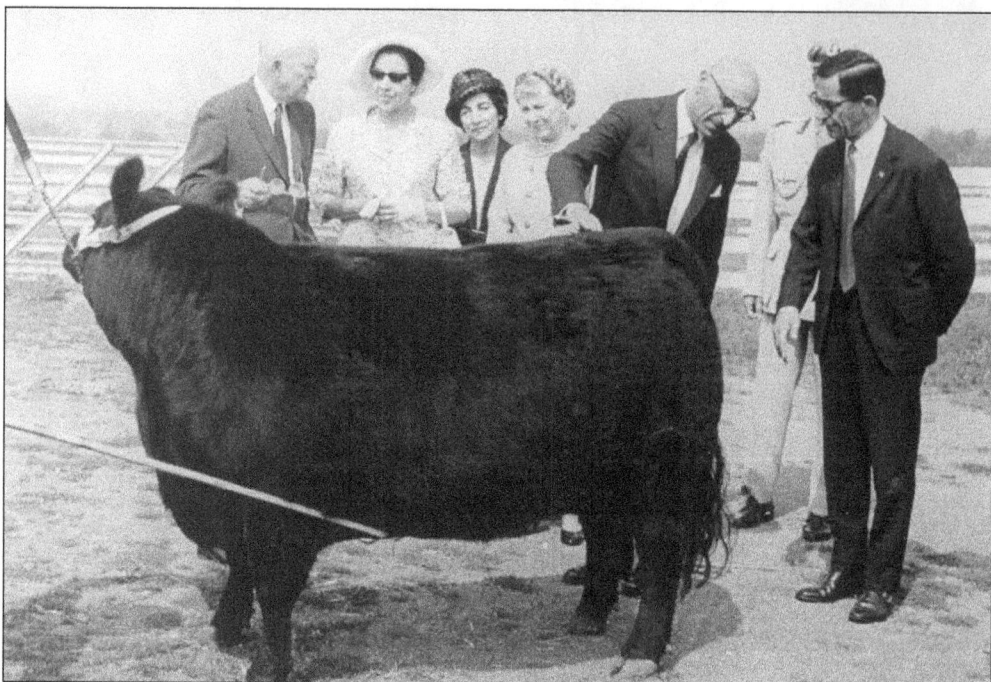

Outside the show barn on Farm 2, Eisenhower explains the finer points of one of his grand champion Angus bulls to King Zahir and Queen Homaira of Afghanistan on their visit to the farm on September 7, 1963. Mamie Eisenhower and others look on. (ENHS1074, BEC.)

Eisenhower talks with Rev. Billy Graham in his office at Gettysburg College on September 29, 1967. Graham had first met with Eisenhower in the White House and continued to meet with him periodically, the last time in December 1968 while Eisenhower was in Walter Reed Army Medical Center. (EL68-106, LS.)

Eight

AN ACTIVE RETIREMENT

Seventy years old when he relinquished the presidency, Dwight Eisenhower might have been expected to focus his energies on his farm and his golf game. In fact, the next seven years represented anything but a textbook retirement. Based in Gettysburg for most of each year (the Eisenhowers spent winters in Palm Desert, California), Ike maintained a remarkably full schedule. His office in the former college president's residence on Carlisle Street in town hummed with activity. Ike continued his active involvement in Republican politics, advised Presidents Kennedy and Johnson on national security affairs, composed several volumes of memoirs and numerous magazine articles, maintained a vigorous correspondence, met foreign and domestic dignitaries, kept tabs on the launching of Eisenhower College in upstate New York, and enjoyed quiet evenings and holidays at the farm with Mamie, his son and daughter-in-law, and the four grandchildren.

During the retirement years, the Eisenhowers were especially close with Art and Ann Nevins, as well as Henry and Peg Scharf. Golf, cocktails, movies, cards, dinner at the Hotel Gettysburg—in various combinations these were part and parcel of the Eisenhowers' social life in the borough. Ike and Mamie participated in services at church, while Ike supported the local American Heart Association fundraising efforts and Republican party events on the local, state, and national levels. Eisenhower also accepted Gettysburg College's invitation to serve on its board of trustees. He took that role seriously enough to attend occasional meetings, make gifts in kind to the college (notably Civil War materials), and participate in the dedication of Musselman Stadium in September 1965.

Early in his retirement, Eisenhower spent much of his day at the office working on his memoirs, together with his son John and former White House aide William B. Ewald. He also collaborated regularly with Ben Hibbs, an editor at the *Saturday Evening Post* and later *Reader's Digest*, producing a series of articles expressing his views on a wide range of current issues. He was constantly in demand as a speaker.

By his 75th birthday in 1965, Ike's health began to wobble, and he decided to "tidy up my affairs somewhat" by selling his Angus herd and paring down his public activity. Evidence suggests, however, that he maintained a substantial schedule of travel and public appearances through the year 1967—his last on the farm.

The Eisenhowers' many friends and admirers looked forward to the couple's return, full-time, to their adopted hometown. One day after the 34th president relinquished his official duties in Washington, Ike was treated to an exuberant welcome home, including a luncheon at the Hotel Gettysburg. Here, on January 21, 1961, Gettysburg College president Gen. Willard S. Paul and Mamie show off a silver tray while Eisenhower displays a plaque made in his honor. (ENHS2026, Paul Roy.)

Eisenhower was a highly popular ex-president, and the daily schedule at his college office on Carlisle Street was full and varied. Here, on May 11, 1961, he meets with former cabinet officers at an informal press conference on the front steps of what is today Gettysburg College's admissions building. Whatever Ike or a member of the press corps said, it evoked great amusement. (ENHS1369, Paul Roy.)

Ike's office at the college was the scene of innumerable meetings and heavy correspondence for nearly seven years. Here, he is depicted seated at work in his comfortable, no-frills second-floor office. (ENHS2425, Paul Roy.)

Much in demand by the media, the former president periodically met with national reporters on issue-related panels and one-on-one interviews. On June 6, 1961, Ike and several Republican officials (including the newly elected Republican senator from Texas, John Tower) sat with NBC television reporter Ray Scherer in the Eisenhowers' backyard for a wide-ranging political discussion. NBC staffers observe at right, one capturing the proceedings with a portable camera. (ENHS2685, LS27456-7.)

Always intense and focused at work, Eisenhower found various ways to relax and kick back. Among his favorite leisure pursuits was painting. Working on the enclosed porch at home in Gettysburg, the former president turned out dozens of portraits and landscapes; many of them became treasured keepsakes of those favored with one or another example of Ike's artwork. Here, Ike contemplates final touches on a portrait completed in July 1966. (EL70-628-119.)

Once settled in their farm property as full-time members of the Gettysburg community, the Eisenhowers, shown here, were regular attendees at the Presbyterian church. They even had their own pew, dating from his presidency. Eisenhower developed a warm relationship with Pastor Robert MacAskill and supported a national fundraising effort by the Presbyterian Church. Mamie contributed as she could to various church-sponsored activities and bazaars. (ENHS2078, ACHS, ZS.)

Eisenhower and Arnold Palmer are pictured on a golf course: perfect together. Palmer was the marquee figure in the world of golf during the Eisenhower era, and Ike was golf's number one ambassador. Palmer and Eisenhower played in foursomes on various occasions, including September 6, 1960, at the Gettysburg Country Club—where according to local lore, Palmer drove the green on the par-4 fifth hole. Here, Palmer, right, observes Eisenhower's swing. Standing with his back to the camera is golf course superintendent Art Kennell, who regularly caddied for Eisenhower. He was cleared by the Secret Service and available during the week whenever Ike wanted to play. A cameraman is visible to the left near the first tee at Gettysburg Country Club. Media could only watch Eisenhower and his guests tee off. They were not allowed to follow them on the course. (Arthur Kennell family.)

This photograph of the Eisenhower family around the dining room table at Thanksgiving takes on special poignancy; it was the last time Ike would participate. By Thanksgiving 1968, he was in frail health, living with Mamie at Walter Reed Army Medical Center in Washington, DC. But November 23, 1967, was great fun. From left to right are Susan, David, Anne, Mamie, Ike, Barbara, Susan's boarding school roommate Amy Hiatt, John, and Mary Jean. (EL70-629-6.)

Contrary to conventional wisdom, it was under Dwight D. Eisenhower that the National Cultural Center (today's Kennedy Center) was conceived and funded. On September 15, 1962, project architect Edward Durrell Stone visited the Eisenhowers at their farm and unveiled a model of his design. (EL64-415, ACHS, ZS.)

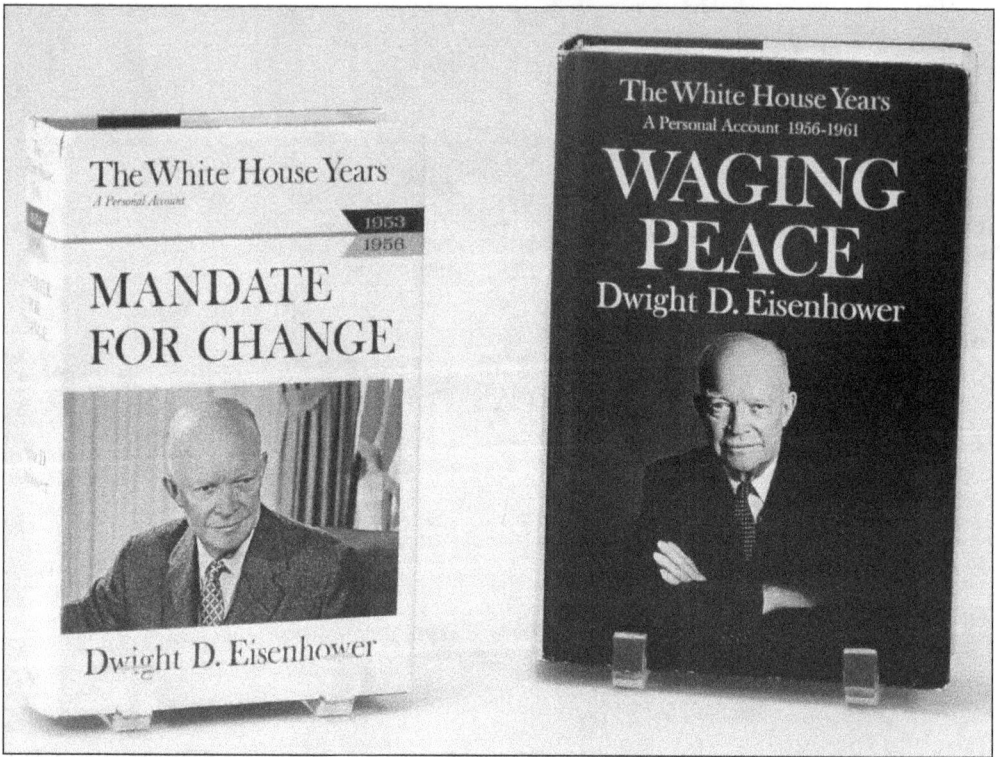

In retirement, Eisenhower's office at Gettysburg College was a beehive of activity on various fronts, but the organizing focus was Ike's presidential memoirs. With the help of son John, pictured below, and former White House aide William B. Ewald, the White House memoirs were researched, composed, edited, and ultimately published by Doubleday in 1963 and 1965, to respectable though not outstanding sales. Ike's life retrospective *At Ease: Stories I Tell to Friends*, published in 1967, became a best seller. (Above, EISE11985/11861, NPS, Museum Management Program, Carol M. Highsmith; below, ENHS2703, LS25883-2.)

Wearing a military hat with the insignia "Honorary National Commander," Eisenhower met with World War I Tank Corps veterans at the Hotel Gettysburg on June 29, 1962. He received a tray from his "Camp Colters" with an engraved tank and the slogan "Treat 'Em Rough." Mamie, her back to the camera, received two dozen red roses. Ike's pleasure at his reunion with his Camp Colt soldiers is obvious. (ENHS2695, LS28602-5.)

It was an honor for Eisenhower to review the band and honor guard at Carlisle Barracks of the Army War College on August 31, 1966, but even more of an honor for that contingent to be reviewed by the organizer of D-day and the defeat of Nazi Germany. That same day, the former president attended a ceremony at the barracks establishing the Eisenhower Chair in National Security Studies. (ENHS2600, LS.)

The first volume of Eisenhower's presidential memoirs, *Mandate for Change*, was published on November 1, 1963. Sales were brisk, but when Pres. John F. Kennedy was assassinated, five days after Ike did a book signing at the Visitor Center in Gettysburg, pictured here, prospects for a best seller plummeted. Americans were less interested in reading about a successful former president than they were in books about a promising president whose life was so tragically cut short. (EL66-19-3.)

When John F. Kennedy declined the invitation to speak in Gettysburg at the centennial ceremonies for the Gettysburg Address, former president Dwight Eisenhower was the natural replacement. Ike spoke to a large crowd on November 19, 1963, in the Soldiers' National Cemetery near where Abraham Lincoln delivered his famous address. Kennedy declined the invitation to visit Dallas, Texas, instead. (ENHS2696, LS30127-9.)

The presidential election of 1964 was a vexation for Eisenhower, not least because conservative firebrand Barry Goldwater defeated Ike's favorite, Pennsylvania governor William Scranton, for the Republican nomination. On September 21, 1964, Goldwater made the obligatory visit to the Eisenhower farm to receive Ike's blessing, but it was too late and too tepid to be of much help to him. He lost in a landslide to incumbent Lyndon B. Johnson. (ENHS2493, PRC.)

Henry Scharf, owner of the Hotel Gettysburg and the Majestic Theater, was one of Eisenhower's closest friends in town. Here, the two men shake hands outside the hotel for the Newspaper Editors Association meeting on June 26, 1962. After leaving the presidency, Eisenhower had to get licensed to drive. Scharf remembered one Saturday Eisenhower parked in front of the hotel. He did not know how to work the parking meter, so Scharf gave Ike a dime. (ENHS3355, GT.)

As a trustee, Eisenhower did his best to be helpful to Gettysburg College. To the delight of a large crowd, Ike helped dedicate Musselman Stadium in September 1965 by throwing a ceremonial first pass. From left to right, looking on appreciatively, are Pennsylvania lieutenant governor Raymond Shafer, college president C. Arnold Hanson, and Gettysburg College athletic director Henry Bream. (GCSC, GEI_0845.)

Meeting with the former president was a treat for scores of young people during Eisenhower's retirement years. Here, he greets members of the Gettysburg College Choir behind his office on the campus around 1967. (GCSC, GEI_0871.)

The Eisenhowers celebrated their 50th wedding anniversary on July 1, 1966. A few days earlier, they sat on an iron bench on the terrace in their backyard for a formal portrait. (ENHS1573, Paul Roy.)

Eisenhower died at age 78 on March 28, 1969. As he lay in state in the Capitol Rotunda in Washington, numerous world dignitaries came to pay their respects, among them French president Charles de Gaulle, with whom Eisenhower had so many meaningful (and often fraught) interactions during World War II and later during Eisenhower's presidency. During the U-2 crisis and the breakup of the Paris summit, de Gaulle made it clear to Eisenhower that the Franco-American bond was unbreakable by stating, "I am with you to the end." (EL71-456-150A, USA, SFC H.P. Palmer.)

Nine

MAMIE

It was her debutante year. Eighteen-year-old Mamie Geneva Doud was being introduced to San Antonio, Texas, society, when on a visit with friends to Fort Sam Houston she met Lt. Dwight Eisenhower. He was known as the post woman-hater. Later, she learned that he liked women but living on the second lieutenant's salary of $141.67 a month made taking women out on dates difficult. When Mamie first set eyes on him, she thought he was the handsomest man she had ever seen, a bruiser, not like all the lounge lizards trying to date her. Ike was equally taken with Mamie, noting her sparkling blue eyes and the saucy look about her. Their relationship, which began with that October meeting in 1915, lasted through 53 years of marriage.

Born in Iowa, Mamie grew up in Denver, Colorado. Her father, John Sheldon Doud, was semiretired from the meatpacking business, and the family was well-to-do. The family home at 750 Lafayette Street was comfortable, with a cook and butler to ease life for her mother, Elivira, and Mamie's sisters, Eleanor, Eda Mae, and Frances. But Eleanor's poor health made spending winters in the warmer climate of San Antonio a necessity.

After dating only four months, Ike proposed. They were married on July 1, 1916, in her home in Denver. For the next 53 years, they lived around the world as Mamie adjusted to the hardships and difficulties of life as an Army wife. She and Ike often entertained their fellow officers and wives, their home garnering the moniker Club Eisenhower. Mamie's skills as a hostess proved invaluable as she supported her husband's rise in rank. She endured many separations from Ike, the loss of their first son, and constant moves—37 times by Mamie's recollection. With all of these experiences, she was well prepared to become first lady when Ike was elected president.

In 1950, after years of having no home of their own, the Eisenhowers purchased their first home, adjoining the Gettysburg battlefield. Finally, Mamie had what she always wanted. She decorated as she liked and unpacked all the furniture she had kept in storage over the years. The home was a place to recharge after illness, visit with family and friends, host world leaders, and just enjoy time with her Ike as husband and wife. After his death in 1969, Mamie continued to live in the Gettysburg home for the last 10 years of her life. She continued to attend the Gettysburg Presbyterian Church, and she supported local causes, such as the fundraising project of Historic Gettysburg-Adams County to brick the sidewalks around the square, signing at least 1,200 cards acknowledging donations.

This 1907 Doud family portrait hangs in the Eisenhowers' Gettysburg home. Pictured are, from left to right, Frances (nicknamed "Mike"), John Sheldon Doud (called "Pupah"), Eda Mae (nicknamed "Buster"), Eleanor, Elivira Carlson Doud (called "Nana"), and Mamie. Pupah wanted some boys, hence the nicknames of the two youngest girls. (ENHS3787.)

Mamie's attire shows her sense of fashion in this 1916 photograph taken at the time of her wedding. She attended Miss Wolcott's Finishing School during the 1914–1915 school year to learn social graces and details of managing a household staff. The following year, she left school to go with her family to San Antonio where she met her future husband. (EL63-51-1.)

Mamie and Icky sit on the steps of the Alpha Tau Omega fraternity house, their housing during the summer of 1918 while Ike was commandant of Camp Colt. Mamie remembered doing dishes in the bathtub as the house had a ballroom on the first floor but no kitchen. When the students returned, the Eisenhowers moved to a house on Springs Avenue. (EL62-340-2.)

During the late 1920s and early 1930s, the Eisenhowers enjoyed a normal family life living at the Wyoming Apartments in Washington, DC. Son John attended grade school across the street, and Mamie drove downtown to shop or rode the trolley. Here, Ike and Mamie pose with John in Rock Creek Park. (EL62-288-1.)

During World War II while Ike was overseas, Mamie lived in the Wardman Park Hotel. She avoided parties and the theater as she felt the supreme allied commander's wife should not be out socializing while soldiers under Ike's command were dying. She stayed in, played cards with friends, and wore her uniform when she volunteered at the Army-Navy-Marine canteen in downtown Washington. (EL66-764, Blackstone Studios.)

Mamie was thrilled when Ike returned from the war. Like most families on the home front, she had spent three years without him, and with their son John at West Point and then overseas with the Army, she was alone for most of it. Here, Mamie and Ike disembark from an airplane as Eisenhower arrives in Washington to report on the war to Congress on June 18, 1945. (HSTL73-1953, NPS, Abbie Rowe.)

In August 1954, while the Eisenhowers' new home was under construction, Mamie invited the wives of cabinet members and friends to see the progress. Mamie, at left, explains the construction of a large picture window for the living room to her guests as they look out the window opening. (ENHS2239, NPS, Abbie Rowe.)

The Eisenhowers' 14-room home was completed in 1955. Coach lamps flanked the front entrance. The stone section housed Eisenhower's den and the guest rooms. Visible above the roofline, the windmill was retained by the Eisenhowers even though it no longer brought water into the home. (ENHS2126, NPS, Abbie Rowe.)

Mamie finishes her snack while playing Scrabble with daughter-in-law Barbara Thompson Eisenhower at Camp David, Maryland. Barbara married Ike and Mamie's son John in 1947. In the distance, Ike and John putt on the golf green. (EL67-83-33, Paul Begley.)

Grandchildren David, Anne, and Susan enjoy supper on the terrace of the main lodge at Camp David on August 1, 1954. Delores Moaney, the Eisenhowers' cook and wife of Sgt. John Moaney, who had served on Eisenhower's personal staff since 1942, assists Susan with drinking her milk and eating her meal. (EL67-83-32, Paul Begley.)

Mamie Eisenhower christens and launches
the USS *Nautilus* at Groton, Connecticut,
on January 21, 1954. As first lady, Mamie was
named the sponsor of the ship. The submarine
was the first to be nuclear powered, breaking
records for longest time and distance submerged.
In 1958, it sailed across the North Pole under
the Arctic icecap. (EL67-71-29U, USN.)

Mamie enjoyed playing cards at the card table
on their glass-enclosed porch. Often, she played
bridge, bolivia, or canasta with her friends.
When alone, her favorite was double solitaire,
which she played while Ike painted at his
nearby easel. She is seen playing cards during
the summer of 1956. (ENHS2092, ANC.)

Mamie was always properly attired as befitted a first lady, with hat, gloves, and purse. In fact, she made the best-dressed list each year she was in the White House. Here, on June 30, 1957, Mamie and Ike sit in auditorium seats while attending the opening program commemorating the anniversary of the Battle of Gettysburg, which took place July 1–3, 1863. (ENHS2069, ACHS, ZS.)

Mamie kisses her mother, Elivera Doud, on the cheek while seated in the backseat of a car on May 14, 1957. A widow, Mrs. Doud spent several months of each year with Mamie at the White House and then returned to Denver. She even had her own bedroom at the Gettysburg farm. (ENHS2739, LS22790-18.)

Standing by the porch outside of her home, the former first lady accepts a ticket to a dinner honoring Republican members of Congress. Pictured here on May 22, 1961, are, from left to right, Clare Brown Williams, Stephanie Miller, Margaret Goldwater, Mamie, Alice Marriott, Helen Westland, and Miriam Summerfield. (ENHS2190, GT, ZS.)

On March 14, 1959, Mamie Eisenhower was awarded an honorary law degree from St. Joseph College in Emmitsburg, Maryland, for her "feminine and matrimonial idealism" and her "staunch fidelity to the Christian ideals of womanhood and marriage." The first lady smiles as Sister Hilda adjusts the hood around her neck while the president looks on. (ENHS3331, GT.)

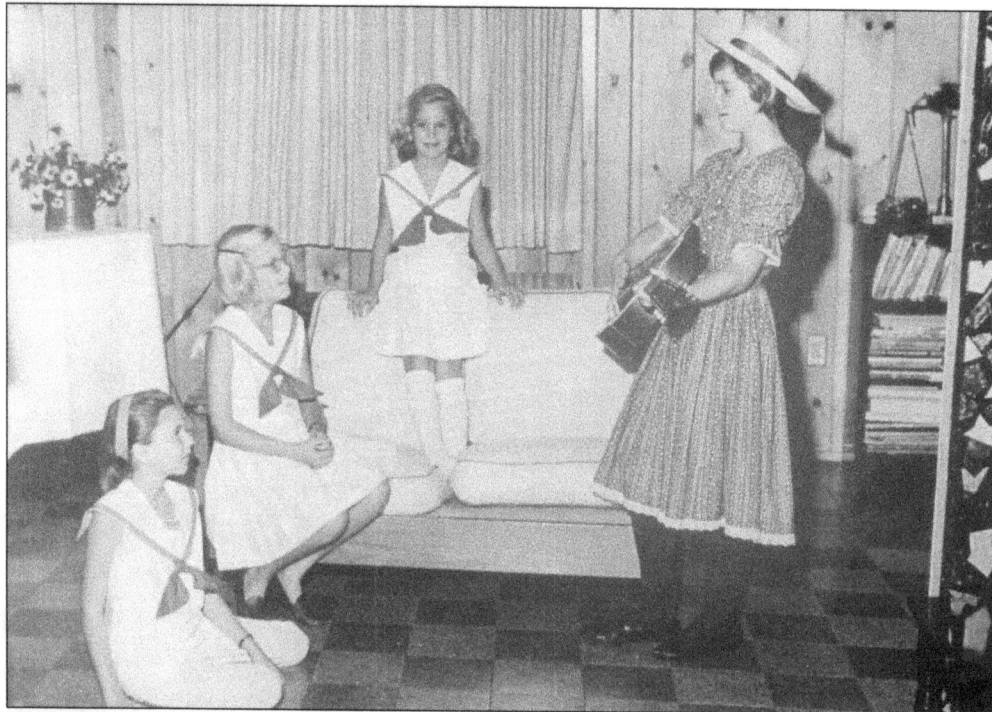

Selecting gifts for the president and first lady was challenging. Daughter-in-law Barbara Eisenhower solved the problem by producing skits with the grandchildren. They did a show called *Young Abe Lincoln*, as well as an elaborate Christmas pageant. The grandchildren even wore lighted halos. Here, in *The Sound of Music*, from right to left, Susan plays Maria, while her sister Mary Jean and friends Nancy Witt and Harriet Barriga play the von Trapp children. They are pictured in October 1963. (ENHS1269, BEC.)

Flanked by geraniums, Mamie poses for the photographer while standing in the open doorway of the porch. She and Ike enjoyed the view into the backyard, with putting green, roses, and cattle in the distant field. (EL70-628-77.)

The Eisenhowers stroll along the terrace behind their home as they pose for photographs marking their 50th wedding anniversary, July 1, 1966. Mamie's father had counseled that marrying an Army man meant constant moves, slow promotions, and low military salaries. She was undeterred, and through it all, their marriage was a success. (ENHS2405, LS32766-11.)

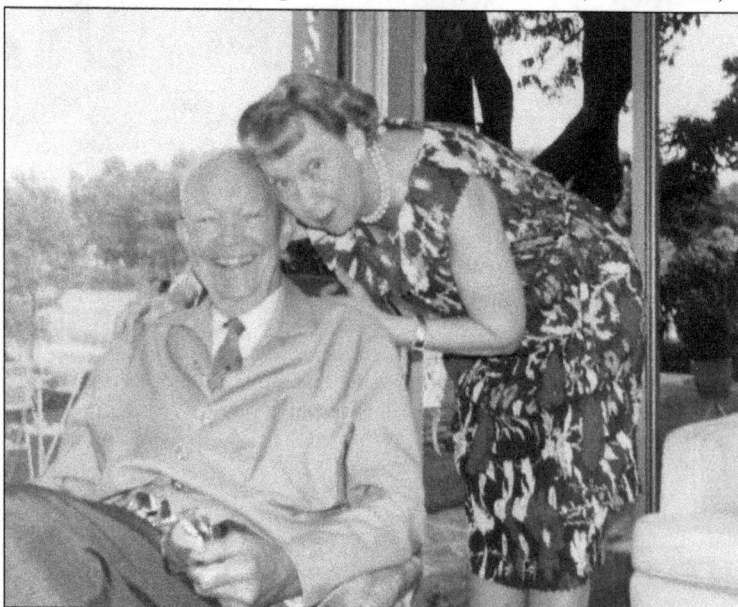

Mamie leans over Ike as he sits in his favorite porch rocking chair in this informal portrait taken in July 1966. Granddaughter Susan remembered Mamie as charming. She charmed even some of the most difficult guests at the White House and farm—a real asset as first lady or a general's wife. (EL70-628-151.)

After Ike's death in 1969, Mamie continued to live at the farm. Family and friends often visited. Here, John Eisenhower sits with his mother on the porch in 1971 amid the Christmas decorations. The lights of the Christmas tree in the living room are visible through the double doors. (ENHS1306, BEC.)

Mamie poses with local residents on the street in Gettysburg. After Ike's death, she continued to attend events and church in town. She also supported the Historic Gettysburg-Adams County effort to brick the sidewalks on the square, personally signing more than 1,200 cards acknowledging donations for each brick. (EL65-407-2.)

In 1969, local Eisenhower associates began an annual commemoration of Eisenhower's birth on October 14. This group founded the Dwight D. Eisenhower Society, which still sponsors the annual event. In 1977, Mamie and grandson David pose after the wreath laying at the Eisenhower statue outside his retirement office on the Gettysburg College campus. (ENHS1311, BEC.)

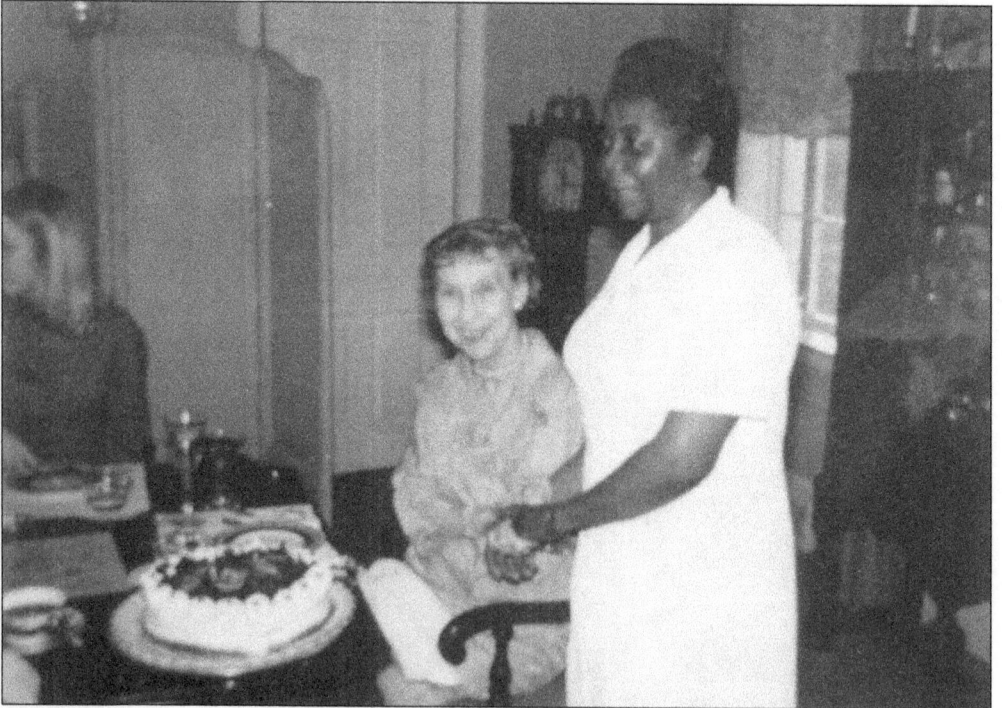

Mamie and Delores Moaney hold hands as the family gathers in 1977 to celebrate their birthdays. Both shared the same birth date 20 years apart; Mamie's was November 14, 1896, and Delores's was November 14, 1916. (ENHS1312, BEC.)

Ten

EISENHOWER NATIONAL HISTORIC SITE

When the secretary of the interior asked General Eisenhower what property associated with his life should be designated a National Historic Landmark, Eisenhower's response was "Our farmstead at Gettysburg . . . because it is the only home, truly ours." In November 1967, the Eisenhowers donated their home and farm to the people of the United States to become the Eisenhower National Historic Site. Eisenhower suffered a third heart attack in May 1968, spending his last 10 months in Walter Reed Army Medical Center, but the farm continued as their primary residence until Ike's death. Mamie did not plan to stay at the farm as a widow. After the general died on March 28, 1969, Mamie changed her mind. Her son John approached the National Park Service on her behalf. A special-use permit was issued allowing Mamie to stay on in the home.

In September 1979, the Secret Service called for an ambulance to the farm. Mamie had a stroke and was transported to Walter Reed Army Medical Center, where she died on November 1, 1979. With her passing, the National Park Service began the process of preparing the site for public visitation.

The National Park Service planned a shuttle system to reduce the impact of vehicular traffic on the site due to the great public interest in touring the home. When the site opened in June 1980, the demand was so high that all shuttle tickets for the entire day were sold by noon. In the first seven months of operation, over 180,000 visitors toured the home and grounds. In addition to the tour of the Eisenhower home, park rangers presented programs on aspects of Eisenhower's life and work. The adjoining farm where Eisenhower raised his registered Angus show cattle was incrementally prepared for visitation as funds allowed. Today, visitation has leveled off at 55,000 to 60,000 annually, but visitors can now enter the cattle barns just as world leaders did when President Eisenhower gave them a tour. Education programs for students, professional development programs for teachers, and special commemorations throughout the year mark events in the Eisenhowers' lives. As the site looks to the future, preservation remains a priority. Daily operations will change with time, and fresh interpretations of Eisenhower's life and work will enrich people's understanding of this iconic American and his beloved Mamie.

Dwight and Mamie Eisenhower present the deed to their farm to Secretary of the Interior Stewart Udall on November 27, 1967. It was a bittersweet moment for Mamie as she quipped she was now living in government housing again. Then the Eisenhowers left Gettysburg for Palm Desert, California. Just before returning to Gettysburg the following spring, Ike had his third heart attack. He spent the last 10 months of his life in Walter Reed Army Medical Center, never to set foot on the farm again. (ENHS2636, USDI, James Aycock.)

On Eisenhower National Historic Site Dedication Day, June 29, 1980, John Eisenhower recollected stories of his parents' life at the farm. Supt. John Earnst listened intently. John Eisenhower inherited the contents of the Eisenhower home from his mother, but his donation of the furnishings to the National Park Service insured visitors would experience the home as his parents had lived in it. (ENHS3567, Arnold, Coughlan.)

With the Eisenhower National Historic Site Dedication Day ceremony concluded, Eisenhower family members enter the house for a visit. From left to right are granddaughter Anne (in plaid dress), daughter-in-law Barbara, son John, and grandson David and his wife, Julie Nixon Eisenhower. (ENHS3507, Arnold, Coughlan.)

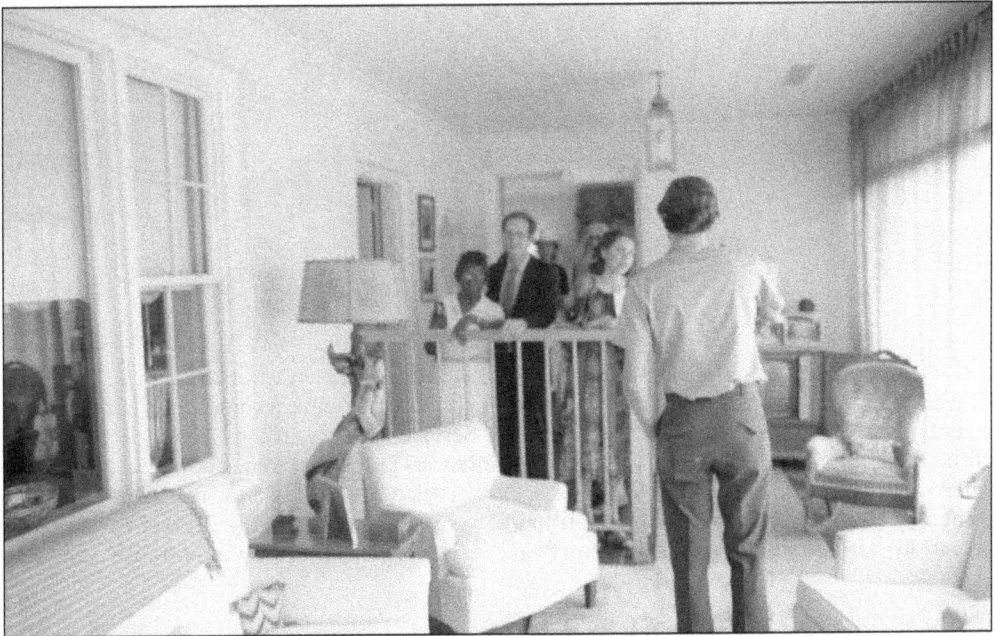

Delores Moaney, David Eisenhower, and Julie Nixon Eisenhower listen as ranger Scott Hartwig answers their questions. Family members and associates shared stories with park staff about life at the farm. Later, the family recollections were captured more formally through oral history interviews. (ENHS3555, Arnold, Coughlan.)

Skeet Range

Equipment Shed

Greenhou

Teahouse

EISENHOWER FARM

Reception Center

Putting Green

Eisenhowe Home

Horse Shelter

Secret Service Office

Barn

Guest House

Orchard

Handicapped parking

Helicopter Landing Pad

Shuttle bus from Gettysburg Visitor Center

North

Scale varies in this perspective view. Background features appear smaller than similar features in the foreground.

Restrooms

Drinking water

The Eisenhower farm encompassed 189 acres with a handsome home, a guesthouse, barn, garden, greenhouses, teahouse, offices for the US Secret Service, and a well-used putting green, a gift of the Professional Golfers Association. The Eisenhowers purchased some additional acreage; so when they donated their farm to the National Park Service, it was 232 acres. Two adjoining farms owned by Eisenhower's partner, W. Alton Jones, were also part of the Eisenhower Farms cattle operation. Barns, loafing sheds, a maternity barn, a semen shed, and, most importantly, the show

FARM 2

Self Feeder

Bull Pen

Show Barn
(Restroom and water available April to October)

Maternity Barn

Loafing Shed

Corn Crib

Hay (barns)

Bull Pen

Garage

Breeding and Tool Shed

Herdsman's Home
(Park Headquarters)

barns

barn were built to support the Eisenhower Farms cattle herd. Farm 2, shown here, was the focal point of the Angus breeding and show cattle operation. Farm 3, not shown, was across the road from the entrance to the tree-lined driveway. It provided additional crop fields and pasture to feed young Angus not selected for the show herd, prior to their sale. All told, the cattle operation encompassed about 495 acres. (NPS, HFC, Chris Casady.)

After the dedication ceremony, public tours of the site resumed. Ranger Todd Bolton, his back to the camera, talks with a group of visitors prior to entering the Eisenhower home. (ENHS3538, Arnold, Coughlan.)

The Eisenhower shuttle bus transported visitors from the National Park Service Visitor Center to the farm and back. A one-way trip took under 10 minutes and departed every 15 minutes. As visitation declined, so did the number of shuttle runs each day. A short audio narration played during the trip to the farm. (ENHS3829.)

The home's living room is filled with gifts the Eisenhowers received, such as the inlaid mother-of-pearl coffee table from the Republic of Korea, the Tabriz rug from the Shah of Iran, and the fireplace mantel that was in the White House during Lincoln's presidency, a gift from the White House staff for their 38th wedding anniversary. (ENHS, Bill Chenaille.)

The porch was the Eisenhowers' favorite room. Here, they entertained friends and family, played cards, watched television shows, and Ike did his oil painting. Soviet premier Nikita Khrushchev, former British prime minister Winston Churchill, and French president Charles de Gaulle all visited here. Ike said he took the measure of the man in this informal setting. (ENHS, Carol Hegeman.)

Wood for beams, wainscoting, and floorboards was salvaged from part of the old house and outbuildings and reused in the den. Here, Ike enjoyed reading and playing cards with friends. Ike also used the sofa bed to take naps while recuperating from his first heart attack in 1955. Each December, Mamie used the den to wrap Christmas presents. (ENHS, Bill Chenaille.)

The Eisenhowers shared the king-size bed in the master bedroom. Mamie said she liked to reach over and pat Ike on his old bald head. It also served as her office, as she often stayed in bed in the mornings propped up on pillows to answer correspondence. The portrait over the fireplace mantel depicts grandchildren David, Anne, and Susan. (ENHS.)

The Eisenhower Reception Center houses a bookstore, a short biographical video, and exhibits on Eisenhower's life and work. Some of the 48,000 artifacts from the Eisenhower museum collection and archive are displayed. (ENHS.)

Park rangers present a variety of interpretive talks and walking tours at the site. Here, ranger John Joyce explains Eisenhower's show cattle operation. Other topics covered by rangers include Eisenhower's military career, his presidency, the role of the Secret Service in protecting the Eisenhowers, and life at the Gettysburg farm. (ENHS, Jankowski.)

Ranger Alyce Evans presents "The Molding of a Leader" character education program to fifth graders visiting the site. Students wear the different hats that Eisenhower wore in his lifetime as they role-play events in his life where he learned good character or exhibited good character. A variety of education programs are presented to students at all grade levels. (ENHS.)

Teachers attending the Eisenhower Academy, a professional development program, tour the historic site with supervisory historian Carol Hegeman. The weeklong program features lectures by scholars on Eisenhower's foreign and domestic policy, 1950s popular culture, and using primary source documents in the classroom. (ENHS.)

Both the Dwight D. Eisenhower Society and the Eisenhower National Historic Site held events to commemorate the centennial of Eisenhower's birth in October 1990. Former president Gerald Ford was the guest speaker at the morning event held at Gettysburg College. (ENHS.)

That afternoon at the farm, a large crowd was welcomed to the centennial commemoration by Supt. Jose Cisneros. The guest speaker was David Eisenhower, seated on the stage to the left of the superintendent. Music by the West Point Glee Club and a landscape restoration by the National Trust for Scotland contributed to the day. (ENHS.)

This US Postal Service first day cover showcases the commemorative Eisenhower postage stamp issued for the Eisenhower centennial. Two cancellations were available—at the Eisenhower Presidential Library in Abilene, Kansas, and at the Eisenhower National Historic Site in Gettysburg, Pennsylvania. (ENHS, EISE 7330.)

Every September, the Eisenhower National Historic Site remembers Eisenhower's role as supreme Allied commander during World War II. Approximately 500 living historians representing the American, British, Polish, French, and Russian allies and regular German army provide demonstrations of equipment and tactics. Authors and veterans speak as well. (ENHS, Richard Lemmers.)

Enjoying their first year of retirement, Mamie and Ike pose on their porch in formal attire before going to their son John and daughter-in-law Barbara's home to celebrate Ike's 71st birthday a day early, October 13, 1961. (ENHS2080, Paul Roy.)

Visit us at
arcadiapublishing.com